What participants and sponsors of Kathy Buys' classes and seminars have to say about Ms. Buys' success at communicating the basics of investing to women:

Seminar sponsors:

"Kathy Buys has taught 'Investment Basics' classes for the City of Aurora Parks and Recreation Department for over 7 years. During this time she has consistently received excellent evaluations from her students.

Kathy is professional, knowledgeable and personable. Her approach is informative while being unintimidating. Her goal is to educate, not sell a product . . . I have great confidence in Kathy's skills and highly recommend her Investment and Financial Seminars."

—Pam Hueseman
City of Aurora Colorado
Parks and Recreation Department
Leisure Lifestyles Program
Supervisor

"Thank you so much for your talk given to our sales group last month. Since your talk, everyone in our group has passed along compliments on what a quality, informative presentation it was that you gave. They were all impressed with your expertise, rationale, and straightforward investment strategies. It is really a pleasure working with you. Thanks again for your time with my group."

—John B. Dickerson
Ortho Pharmaceutical Corporation
Manager, Denver District

"As always, you entertained us and informed us with your lively, insightful presentation on the financial market and current investment strategy. We will be looking forward to your video and forthcoming book."

"The feedback to your presentation was very positive, and I had several employees who were unable to attend approach me after the session to ask when we would be scheduling another presentation. I am certain these employees were responding to comments from the employees who were able to attend. On behalf of the firm, thanks again for the terrific presentation."

"As program director, I have always found Kathy a delight to work with. She is brimming with ideas about how to develop her classes and make them more fun-filled and informative. She has a sincere interest in making her time with students a terrific educational experience."

"Thank you for your wonderful presentation to our staff. One employee obtained a copy of your video, and others have asked me about your book. When your book is available, we would like information on how to buy it. Several people would like to purchase copies. We greatly appreciate your efforts in helping to educate our staff in the area of investing."

"Kathy was very helpful to me during our recent plant shut-down. I especially appreciate that during a very busy and trying time for me, all I had to do was introduce Kathy to the employees at the seminar, and she took over from there. She was sensitive, helpful, and instrumental in helping employees shift their attention away from the anger of losing their jobs to planning for their new futures."

Students:

"Kathy's no nonsense approach and ability to demystify the stock market and investing are the high points of the workshop."

"Kathy has a great sense of humor and makes hard material understandable and interesting."

"There are doubtless many who have the knowledge of your world that Kathy does, but few, I am sure, who can teach it. Kathy has a gift of being able to take complex principles and make them lucid to beginners."

"I have never learned so much from one class ever!! I could have listened to Kathy for several more hours."

"Informative, entertaining, clear and understandable. I could have sat for another several hours."

"Kathy Buys is gifted as a speaker and is the first person in 38 years who penetrated my thick skull and even made me enjoy learning about investing. I have never taken a class more organized, more concise, and more to the point."

"I wish Kathy would have been my economics teacher—with her explanations I would have gotten more out of college."

"I now feel capable of making informed investment decisions because of this class."

"It totally exceeded my expectations. Kathy didn't talk down to us, making this an extremely worth while class."

"Kathy is humorous, knowledgeable and a very talented teacher. She gave an excellent introduction to investments."

"Kathy has a great sense of humor and a down to earth approach."

"This was the best class I've ever had—including college. I could have stayed all day."

"Kathy explains plain and simply—great!"

"What did I like most about the class? Boy, do I know more now!"

"Great information! Thanks for relating it to me instead of using the jargon."

"The best part of the class was how well Kathy described something that previously had seemed overwhelming to me."

"Kathy Buys' personality kept this class interesting. I left encouraged, empowered and enthused! She gave great explanations. I never thought I'd "get" this stuff, but I "got" it. I'm NOT stupid!"

"Down to earth talk, but not talked down to."

"Kathy has a great sense of humor and an ability to explain technical jargon in layman's terms."

"Kathy gave simple explanations to complicated ideas."

"Enjoyed Kathy and her focus and understanding of women's experiences and backgrounds."

"Outstanding! I didn't think I would understand a thing, but I did. Write the book!!!"

"It's clear that not only does Kathy have superior technical knowledge, but also a rare gift for expressing herself in a crystal clear manner. It was a pleasure—thank you!"

Investment BASICS *for* WOMEN

THE ESSENTIAL GUIDE TO TAKING CONTROL OF YOUR FINANCES

by

KATHY BUYS

and

JONATHAN BEROHN

MACMILLAN SPECTRUM/ALPHA BOOKS
A Division of Macmillan General Reference
A Simon and Schuster Macmillan Company
1633 Broadway, New York, NY 10019-6705

International Standard Book Number: 0-02-861175-6
Library of Congress Catalog Card Number: 96-078159

98 97 96   8 7 6 5 4 3 2 1

Interpretation of the printing code: the rightmost double-digit number is the year of the book's first printing; the rightmost single-digit number is the number of the book's printing. For example, a printing code of 96-1 shows that this copy of the book was printed during the first printing of the book in 1996.

Printed in the United States of America

Publisher: Theresa Murtha

Editor in Chief: Dick Staron

Production Editor: Whitney K. Ward

Cover Designer: Heather Kern

Designer: Heather Kern

Indexer: Alex Zane

Production Team: Douglas & Gayle Ltd.

Contents

Introduction

By picking up this book, you've already validated my belief that women want to learn about investing, and they want to take charge of their own financial futures. As a financial advisor and as a woman, I feel a strong obligation to help women enter the often intimidating world of investing. When I first set out to teach a course called *Investment Basics for Women*, I had a hard time finding any takers among the local continuing education outlets.

"Women aren't interested in investing," was the standard reply. These negative responses were polite but nevertheless insulting and disturbing. I wasn't discouraged, though. The attitudes reflected by the heads of these programs—all men, interestingly enough—just reinforced my belief in the need for basic investment information geared toward women. Fortunately, I found a forum for my class at an adult education center that was willing to take a chance on me . . . and the women of Denver proved me right. That was five years ago, and now the class almost always has a waiting list!

I shouldn't take all the credit, though, for coming up with the idea for the class and now for this book. Early in my career, my experiences with women investors jolted me into taking action to help women help themselves. The stories of a few of these women stand out in my mind and continually remind me of why I want to help. Listen to them, and see if they remind you of anyone you know.

In any brokerage firm, the brokers dutifully take their turn as broker of the day. (Brokerage firms sell investments, and brokers do the selling.) Since the broker of the day gets the first crack at any new walk-in clients, no one finds this assignment much of a burden. Once during my early years when I was broker of the day, a woman came into the office with a fistful of statements in her hand asking to speak to someone.

She was a soft spoken elderly woman whose husband had recently died. He had always assured her that she didn't have to worry about finances, that he'd take care of everything. And if anything should happen to him, he'd told her, she should see their accountant, Charlie, because he had handled their finances for years. Unbelievably, shortly after her husband was buried, Charlie had a massive stroke that totally incapacitated him and left this woman with no one to turn to for help.

As luck would have it, she saw the name of my firm on one of her statements, and she came into my office, confused and carrying an armload of papers. She came in, sat down, handed the whole pile over to me, and said, "Is this any good?" It turned out that she had a strong portfolio full of excellent holdings, and we really didn't need to do much to adjust it to her needs and objectives.

But imagine if she had happened upon a broker—and don't kid yourself, they're out there—who was just a little bit unscrupulous. She might have been told that her investments, "while excellent in past years when her husband had purchased them, had proven risky with the current market conditions." The broker might have also said she'd be "much better off with the in-house mutual fund since it gained 15% last year," not to mention the extra rewards the broker may get for selling it. If you're not sure what I'm talking about, think how you would feel if you went to any financial advisor uninformed.

I've found that most women generally—though this is changing—aren't expected to take much of a part in investing and finance. And traditionally, women certainly aren't expected to understand any of it even if they decide to get involved. Women hear this mantra so much in life that, unfortunately, many women begin to believe it. Even during seminars I conducted at Fortune 500 companies, the women who had come early, armed with insightful questions and flashing keen interest, disappeared into the potted plants when the men arrived. They just didn't believe that they understood finance as well as men. And that's where the real problems begin.

Once I realized this, I began to notice more and more women coming to me after a divorce, the death of a spouse, or simply out of concern for their finances. Often, these women had no knowledge of what, if anything, they already owned; no experience in making financial decisions; and no idea where to begin. These women weren't stupid; they'd just never been expected to handle these kinds of affairs, and suddenly when they needed to, they had no experience or knowledge to go on. They either had to put all their faith (and money) in the hands of a financial advisor or miss out entirely on investment opportunities simply because they didn't know how to recognize them.

If I haven't already gotten your attention, here's another example of how damaging a lack of knowledge about finances can be. A woman came to me with a truly tragic story. When her husband died, she didn't know how to take over the family finances. She was a bright, college-educated woman in her fifties, but her husband had handled all their financial affairs. He did a pretty good job, though, and left her with enough assets to ensure that she would be able to continue to fund her two children's college expenses while maintaining her lifestyle.

Unfortunately, when she received her husband's substantial life insurance settlement, she didn't have a clue as to what to do with the money. She knew her husband had worked with a financial planner in the past, so she turned to him. This planner convinced her that she could get a very good return on this lump sum of money if she purchased a sizable business loan. She assumed this loan was secured, but she didn't ask. Not only was the loan unsecured, but it turned out to be nothing more than a slush fund, or scheme, so that the planner could move to Florida.

The payments stopped soon after her advisor relocated. Even the private detective she hired couldn't get any money out of him. The planner knew a lot more about keeping the money from her than she did about protecting it for herself. To this day, she has recovered very little of this money, and she's found herself sinking from financial security to financial crisis without ever knowing what happened.

Often, women use examples like these to justify "excessive caution"—the other common pitfall of women investors. Women tend to be risk averse and don't like to take chances, especially with money. Women generally pay attention to what their gut tells them. Most of the time, relying on this is all right except with regard to market-related investments. Many times when our gut is telling us to sell, we should in fact be doing the exact opposite—buying.

Thinking long-term and not reacting to the normal, although upsetting, pullbacks in the market are vital to investment success. While there's a good deal to be said for playing it safe, if you're too safe you'll miss the boat. In fact, you can actually see your hard-earned savings shrink in value over the years as it gets eaten away by taxes and inflation while it's locked away in a savings account or Certificate of Deposit (CD). Don't be like one client of mine who insisted she needed $40,000 in her savings account because she thought she might have to buy a new washer and dryer soon. Learn about investing. Learn what's out there. Learn to make your money work for you.

More importantly, learn to do something *now*! It doesn't matter if you've just started your first job or you're already retired. You need to start getting the most from your money no matter what stage of life you're in. Young women are in the best position to get off to a head start to invest for their futures. Unfortunately, they're also the least likely to start investing because retirement is so far away that it doesn't seem real, and they have plenty of other demands on their money right now. Don't let this happen to you.

While investing may sound expensive, you don't have to start off with a lot of money. As you'll see later in this book, an investment as small as $50 a month adds up to a nice nest egg over the long haul. Even for those of us who are not sweet, young things, the same rules apply. You must make sure your money is working as hard for you as you are for your money. It's never too late to start.

When you finish this book, you'll have a basic understanding of the investment world and most common types of investments so you won't make the mistake of waiting too long. If you're already an experienced trader, you'll probably be disappointed that you're not going to learn how to buy pork bellies and gold futures or learn all the subtleties and nuances of every investment category. Still, this book will make definitions of investments and investment jargon as simple and unintimidating as possible. You won't find any hot tips on how to get rich quick, but you will get a solid foundation of financial understanding. Then you can use this knowledge to take advantage of the financial opportunities that are available for everyone.

To provide some practical applications to the definitions and basic information presented in this book, anecdotes based on students in my Investment Basics classes are included at the end of most of the chapters.

Also, I've enlisted the help of a fictional "Lynn." Lynn is a 40-year-old woman with two children who's just gotten divorced. Her husband had handled all of the finances during their marriage, and now she has to take over, but she doesn't have the slightest idea where to begin. Lynn will make an appearance at the end of the book to give you a realistic example of what I've been throwing at you. Hopefully, she'll also liven this up a little bit. I know that my usual attention span for an investment book lasts until the commercial break is over, so I'll try to keep things moving along.

Acknowledgments

To my friend and co-worker,

Heidi Schoenberger,

without whom this book literally could not have been written in any way, shape, or form.

Facing *the* CHALLENGE

This is what I like to call my "dose of reality" chapter. Sometimes we need a good dose of reality to wake us up, shock us out of our comfort zones, and make us focus on the things that benefit us in the long run. In this chapter I'm going to give you a lot of numbers to chew on and a lot of facts to think over. I'm going to show you why you need to invest and what's waiting for you if you don't. Hopefully, this information will motivate you to see how powerful you are and how critical it is to use the financial tools available to you.

Whenever I teach a new class of women, I always start off with a few simple questions. First, I ask how many people own any stock. A few people raise their hands. Second, I ask how many people own any bonds. A few scattered hands go up. Next, I ask how many people own mutual funds. A few more hands. Finally, I ask how many people don't know what they own. Everybody always laughs at that one, and that's one of the reasons I ask it, but almost everybody usually raises their hand, too. This is precisely the problem we have to address.

We all know that money is too important to ignore. We all work, agonize over our spending habits, and try to save a little for the future. However, what most of us don't realize is that simply *saving* money is not enough. We need the money to grow so that when we want to start a new business, go to college, or retire, there will be enough to cover our needs. And, the only way to get your money to grow is to invest it. In order to effect the kind of growth that is needed to outpace inflation and provide enough income for future needs, you must first understand the basics of money and the many investment options available.

TIME TO TAKE CHARGE

By choice or by default, men have traditionally assumed the financial responsibilities in American households. This role may have worked when the majority of women were stay-at-home housewives. I don't need to remind you that things have changed, and that now you'll find far more women who work outside the home than don't. Women have become full partners in earning the household income, but we aren't full partners in managing it!

Don't get me wrong. I'm not saying women aren't interested in investing. I *know* women are interested in investing. Women make up the overwhelming majority of my clients, and they fill my classes until there are waiting lists for available spots. The major brokerage houses and mutual fund companies know women are interested in investing too. They're spending millions of dollars to tap into the women's market.

So why aren't women full partners in the world of investing? You probably know the answer to that already. Let's face it, finances can be intimidating and downright scary. And, to make matters worse, many male financial advisors reinforce these fears. These advisors are used to meeting and dealing with male clients, and most of us don't fit nicely into their ways of doing business.

Based on my experience, many male brokers, and some female brokers for that matter, have canned speeches or presentations ready to pitch particular products or investment plans. Male clients may feel comfortable with a quick yes or no and instant decisions, but women often want more information and more time to deliberate before making an investment decision. We want to know why certain products fit our needs, and we want to take the time to consider whether or not an investment fits into our plan goals.

But rather than tailor their approaches to help women feel more comfortable, many brokers seem to almost go out of their way to make women uneasy. When a male client asks a male broker questions, the client is almost always taken seriously. If, on the other hand, a woman asks these same questions, there's a good chance the broker will be patronizing and condescending, often leaving the women even more intimidated about investing.

Women have different financial needs and agendas than men. Men generally believe that they will be able to handle money and investments. Women generally believe they won't. Many men feel that if they lose money in an investment they'll be able to make it up in a future investment. Women, on the other hand, are often so fearful of making the wrong investment choice that they make no investment choices at all. Men who invest successfully tend to give themselves the credit. Men whose investments fail tend to blame outside sources such as changing market conditions. A woman with a successful investment often credits her financial advisor's sage advice and blames herself if an investment goes wrong.[1] Most financial advisors just aren't prepared to explain or interested in addressing these differences.

If you turn your money over to any financial advisor, let alone a traditional male-oriented advisor, with no idea of what you want to do and no understanding of financial markets and investments, you could be asking for trouble. You won't know what questions to ask, and even if your advisor gives you all the information you need, you won't know how to use it. I'm not trying to suggest that all financial advisors would take advantage of your lack of knowledge for their own substantial gain. Things like that do happen though, and unfortunately, we hear about them more than we hear about sound investment advice.

What will happen, according to a survey in *Money* magazine's June 1994 issue, is disturbing enough. Brokers at the large firms that the magazine surveyed spent considerably more time with their male clients, presented a far wider range of potential investments to their male clients, and lumped virtually all of the women into low-risk, low-return investments regardless of their individual financial positions. This bias is so widespread that the Chairman of the House Finance Subcommittee has asked the Securities and Exchange Commission (SEC) to conduct an inquiry into the treatment of women by brokerage houses.[2]

By walking into a financial advisor without knowing what to expect, what to ask, or what to avoid, you're telling the advisor that these stereotypes are accurate. You're sending a signal that you don't understand investing and you don't want to learn, when, in fact, you may be the most curious and inquisitive investor they'll ever come across. The trouble is they've been conditioned to think that women don't want to be bothered with money matters, and you've been conditioned not to question this because you're afraid of looking dumb.

---

[1] "Caveat Gender," *Olivia Mellan, Dow Jones Investment Advisor*, June 1996.

[2] *Bank Investment Marketing*, July-August 1994.

However, unless all women take active steps to educate ourselves and assert our needs, we will continue to be put in the safest, quickest, and least rewarding investments the brokers can find so they can get back to their male clients—the "serious" investors. All the while, they'll be thinking they're doing us some kind of favor by shielding us from the complexities and risk of real investing.

At the same time that we're getting slighted by the financial world, we're also still yielding to men's "better judgment" at home. Women now earn more than $1 trillion every year, and over 300,000 women have incomes of more than $100,000.[1] Those are powerful figures. We're working pretty hard out there and making a lot of money. Right now there are 58 million women in the work force, and that number is growing faster than any other group.[2] But still, men control the financial decisions in most households. We still think that after we sweat and slave away for our money, we'll be best off if we then happily turn our paychecks over to our husbands to take care of all the messy decisions involved with money so we don't have to worry about them.

Wrong! Fifty-four percent of all marriages end in divorce these days. That means one out of every two married women will suddenly find themselves solely responsible for every decision for themselves and their families including finances. So, if you're one of those women, and you left all of the financial decisions to your husband, you need to start getting a handle on your finances now.

Even if you're lucky enough to marry the greatest guy in the world, who also happens to be a financial whiz, you still need to be involved in managing your money. The simple truth is that women live longer than men. In fact, the average age of widowhood is 56.[3] As our life expectancy nears 90, you can expect to live in retirement nearly 25% longer than men.[4] In fact, when you factor in divorce and women who choose to stay single, one way or another most women end up alone: 85% of women die single.[5] There will come a time in most women's lives when there's no one else to turn to, and they'll have to make all of the decisions. I know I wouldn't be too comfortable thinking about that and realizing I didn't know the first thing about money.

---

[1] U.S. Bureau of Labor Statistics, 1993

[2] U.S. Department of Labor

[3] "Tips about Social Security," Life Planning for Women, Inc.

[4] U.S. National Center for Health Statistics, 1993

[5] "Message for Women Is Clear: Strive for Financial Independence," Paula Voell, *Buffalo News*, August 17, 1994.

And that's exactly the dilemma that most women will face. Often, young girls are discouraged from delving into finance. How many Nobel Prize–winning female economists can you think of? Do you think that's an accident? I sure don't. Money is still a man's realm, or at least men think it is. But what's worse is how many women think it is, too.

We're so used to being told that finance is too complicated for us that we're more than a little willing to keep out of anything to do with investing. We begin to think that finance and investment are as difficult, obscure, and risky as we are led to believe, and we shy away from anything to do with money that's not a savings account or a CD. Couple this attitude with the traditional lack of financial training that women receive, and it's no wonder that studies like Oppenheimer Management's 1992 survey consistently find that women know less about money management than men: 89% of women surveyed (vs. 69% of men) had no idea what the level of the Dow Jones Industrial Average was; 77% (65% for men) didn't understand the relationship between interest rates and bonds; and 69% (53% for men) didn't know that stocks have historically outperformed bonds, CD's, and money markets.[1]

If you follow my sample class and read through this book, you'll learn what you need to know to level out the investment playing field. You'll be able to understand advice you might seek out, and you'll know if your financial advisors are recommending what's good for *you* or good for *them*. Most important, you'll know how to get involved. And if you stay involved in your family finances, chances are you'll never be caught by surprise without any investment savvy to fall back on. Knowing what's going on is always important with investing.

For women, though, faced with the almost certain prospect of being alone at some point in our lives, it's more important than ever that we understand how to manage our finances. Then, and only then, can we be sure that our money's working as hard for us as we've worked for it.

How Much Money Do I Need to Invest?

Perhaps the biggest misperception about investing that I see is a feeling that you don't have enough money to invest. I find this view especially widespread among younger women, who are typically still paying off student loans or are just starting out in their profession. In reality, though, there's almost no such thing as not having enough money

---

[1] "Buoying Women Investors," Pam Black, *Business Week*, February 27, 1995.

to invest. Younger women in particular are missing out on a great chance to invest seemingly insignificant amounts of money because they've got the time to let these small investments grow.

Let's look, for example, at some figures for a 25-year-old woman who wants to invest for her retirement at age 60.

MONTHLY INVESTMENTS YIELDING 8% BEGINNING AT AGE 25

Monthly Investment	Total Investment Value at age 60
$25.00	$57,348
$50.00	$114,694
$100.00	$229,388

As you can see, investing $100 a month at 8% yields quite a tidy sum over 35 years. Even if you can't afford $100 a month, though, $50 and $25 monthly investments still bring quite a return over 35 years.

Now I know most of you who are reading this aren't 25, but you still don't need to give up hope if you can't afford expensive investments. Let's look at the same $25-, $50-, and $100-a-month investments, but let's change things a little and look at a 30-year-old woman and a 35-year-old woman.

MONTHLY INVESTMENTS YIELDING 8% BEGINNING AT AGE 30

Monthly Investment	Total Investment Value at age 60
$25.00	$37,259
$50.00	$74,518
$100.00	$149,036

MONTHLY INVESTMENTS YIELDING 8% BEGINNING AT AGE 35

Monthly Investment	Total Investment Value at age 60
$25.00	$23,776
$50.00	$47,551
$100.00	$95,103

Again, the results of these "small" investments look pretty good if we let them work over the long haul. You'll also notice, however, how important it is to get started. Every day you wait to invest is money lost over the long haul.

I'm sure at least some of you are saying to yourselves, "Sure, those figures look good, but how am I going to average 8% with $25, $50, or $100 a month?" We're going to delve deeply into that question as we focus on types of investments and investment strategy. Right now, though, let me give you a real life example of a young woman who's a client of mine, and who's well on her way to securing her financial future. Let me warn you right now that you probably won't know what some or all of the investments in this example are. Don't worry, we'll cover them all in future chapters. For right now, though, they'll still show you how easy it is to invest, even with limited resources, and they'll also show you how easy it is to get lost if you don't know the basics.

This young woman, let's call her Carol for the sake of this example, is a 29-year-old single female who has never made more than $30,000 a year. Carol made her first investment at the age of 24 when she put $500 in a mutual fund and bought 10 shares of stock. She hopes to use this investment to buy a house in the near future. At 25, Carol started planning for her retirement by starting an IRA with $250 in another mutual fund and also contributing 8% of her salary to her company's 401(k) retirement plan, with the company matching the first 4%.

Now, 5 years after her first investment, Carol's assets have grown to $3,500 in cash, $1,200 worth of stocks, and $2,600 in a mutual fund. Carol's IRA, rolled over from her old company's retirement plan (we'll cover that later), is currently worth $25,000, and her new retirement plan is already worth $1,200. Remember, Carol earned all this in 5 years' time on salaries of less than $30,000! The simple moral to this story is never let a broker tell you you're wasting your time with small investments. You can only waste your own money by not investing it.

CLASS NOTES

Almost everyone who comes to my classes is nervous, to some degree, especially after hearing so many horror stories about investing. Before even starting the class, I must make everyone feel comfortable. I understand their fears and try to establish an atmosphere in which the women can see they're not alone and can feel they'll learn enough to be able to help themselves.

When the students sit down and skim through the class material, I know that some of the women start to feel uneasy, but then they start looking around. They see other women: young, middle-aged, older women from all sorts of economic backgrounds. They don't know the other women or anything about each other, but they see twenty anxious faces on women apprehensive but eager to dive into the "mysterious" world of finance. They see themselves.

Inevitably, when they realize this they begin to believe that they belong. They all began to relax, and one brave soul slowly raises her hand with a question. "This class is for beginners, right?"

"Absolutely!" I say. "I'll guarantee you right now that you'll walk out the door tonight knowing a whole heck of a lot more than you do now. And in fact, most of you will be comfortable enough to start making some investment decisions.

"I know," I continue, "that most of you are wondering what I smoked before I came here tonight, but for now, trust me on this." They all laugh. "We're going to see that there are a few, basic, easy-to-understand rules that you need to keep in mind when looking at investments. We're going to stick to the basics— none of the fancy terminology and weird investment strategies that you'd never use—and we'll keep it informal. Ask me any question you want to ask . . . as long as it's not too personal, of course."

So, the first hurdle is behind us.

2 Why Do I *need* TO INVEST?

THE SAVINGS ACCOUNT TRAP

If you pay even a limited amount of attention to your money, you may have been confused about what I said in the last chapter regarding Certificates of Deposit and savings accounts. After all, CD's, savings accounts, and similar accounts guarantee you a fixed return and are the safest places to put your money. While this is true, it's even more important that you stay aware of the two biggest hurdles that all investments have to overcome: taxes and inflation. When you factor in the money you lose to taxes and inflation, then savings accounts and CD's start to lose their shine.

A FUTURE NEED is an anticipated goal or event that will require a large sum of money.

Before I explain the nuts and bolts of investments that will enable you to outpace inflation and taxes, you should first understand why it's important to put money away rather than spend every penny on new cars, clothes, and vacations.

Investment Goals

The two most common reasons people save money are future need and retirement. Maybe you've been thinking of starting your own business. (By the year 2000, women will start 50% of all small businesses.[1]) Likewise, if you plan on buying a house or sending your kids to college, you're going to need money. That's future need.

When asked about their biggest fear in life (other than dying), Americans consistently and overwhelmingly respond that it's outliving their money. You'll need to take care to look out for yourself if you want to enjoy a comfortable retirement. The National Center for Women and Retirement Research reports that even including Social Security, the median annual income of women over 65 is $7,300. You don't need me to tell you that's not enough to live on.

Still, many women simply don't plan for their retirement. It's not surprising then to learn that women make up 75% of the elderly poor. Forget about early retirement—if you want to be able to simply live without worrying about day-to-day expenses, you need to supplement that $7,300. In order to assure that you can continue to enjoy your quality of life, you need to put money aside, and you need to start doing it today!

Rules of the Game

Both future need and retirement have something in common—you can't pay for them now, so you hope to save enough money to be able to afford them later. The longer lead-in period you have, the more money you can amass. The driving force behind all this goes back to your desire to have as much money as possible when it comes time to pay for that college education or move to Florida to play golf. It's only natural, therefore, to want to see the money you put away grow to as large a sum as possible. That's not going to happen if you keep it in CD's and savings accounts.

This simple message is worth repeating: keeping all your money in savings and CD's is not going to get you the nest egg you need. Here's why savings accounts and CD's come up short.

INVESTMENT RETURN

To get a better understanding of how much money you actually make from savings, or any investment, consider what is known in the financial world as "rate of return."

---

[1] "Women and Retirement: The Harsh Realities," Christopher L. Hayes, Best's Review, July 1991.

A $10,000 CD paying 5% interest makes a simple example. That CD has a rate of return of 5%, meaning you will earn an interest payment of 5% of $10,000, or $500. If you make money, the rate of return is positive. If you lose money, the rate of return is negative. Rate of return is usually expressed in terms of a percentage of how much money you invested, also known as the principal.

> The **RATE OF RETURN** on any investment is the amount of money you earn.

For a savings account or CD, the principal would be how much money you originally deposited. The principal in the $10,000 CD in our example is $10,000. That's how much you invested. For stocks, bonds, and other types of investments, the principal is how much money that investment cost you to buy. Obviously, you can make a withdrawal, deposit more money, or buy more stocks over time. When you do that, you change your principal. With that in mind, rate of return is usually calculated over the period of one year with this simple equation:

> The **PRINCIPAL** for any investment is how much money you initially spend on that investment.

$$Rate\ of\ Return = \frac{(money\ at\ the\ end\ of\ 1\ year - principal)}{principal}$$

The rate of return can be calculated by updating the value of your investment. The equation gets more involved if you add money throughout the year, but don't worry about this for the moment. Here's an example to make this clear:

If someone made 4% on his or her investment last year, the return was 4%. That's simple enough. You can also calculate the rate of return for that investment if you know that the investor started with $100 and ended up with $104.

$$\frac{104-100}{100} = \frac{4}{100} = Rate\ of\ Return = 4\%$$

Let's keep going with this and assume our investor kept her money in the same investment for another year. At the start of year 2, she had $104. At the end of year 2, she had $109. Let's figure out the new rate of return.

$$\frac{109-104}{104} = \frac{5}{104} = Rate\ of\ Return\ for\ Year\ 2 = 4.8\%$$

The rate of return is important to know when you're considering where to put your money. Obviously you would like the highest return possible. If you want to put your money in a CD, you're going to find out which bank offers the highest rate of return. As good as that may sound, though, rate of return doesn't give you the full picture of how much you're going to earn from your investment.

REAL RATE OF RETURN is the value of an investment's return after subtracting inflation.

In financial circles, the "real rate of return" is what matters. This gives investors a general idea of what to expect from an investment. Real rate of return, however, is a general figure that, while it does compensate for inflation, doesn't take taxes into account. So again, real rate of return is a somewhat incomplete number. To find out the best indicator of how an investment will perform, you have to go one step further and calculate the "effective rate of return," which is how much money you actually see from your investment.

EFFECTIVE RATE OF RETURN is the value of an investment's return after subtracting taxes and inflation.

Simply put, effective rate of return is the rate of return less taxes and inflation. Another way to look at it is that effective rate of return is what you get (rate of return) minus what you give away (inflation and taxes). Here's another simple equation that lets you calculate effective rate of return:

Effective Rate of Return = Rate of Return - (taxes + inflation)

Taxes & Inflation

The impact of taxes and inflation on investments is substantial. Almost all income is taxable. Every penny of interest you earn from a normal savings account is taxable, assuming that you're over age 18. Taxes, of course, aren't limited to savings income—income from most investments is taxable. There are of course some tax-free investments, but this discussion will focus on taxable savings compared to other taxable investments. Even if you're making the 4% on your savings account from the example up above, you end up paying, on average, 28% of your interest income in taxes in the middle tax bracket. If the government is taking 28% of your 4% interest, that's 1.12% that you don't get. You only get 72% of your interest, or a 2.88% return on the principal.

Taxes on Return = Return x Tax Rate = 4% x 28% = 1.12%

Return after Taxes = 4% -1.12% = 2.88%

On a return of $1,000, taxes knock what you actually get down to $720.

Taxes on $1,000 Return = $1,000 x 28% = $280

Return after Taxes = $1,000-$280 = $720

That's before taking inflation into account!

When economists talk about inflation, they are really talking about prices. Everybody's parents or grandparents love to say, "When I was a kid, we used to go to the movies for a quarter." Obviously, you can't do that today. You're lucky to find a movie for $7 or less. This is inflation. You still get the same product you used to get, but you have to pay more for it. In economic terms, your "purchasing power" has gone down.

> **INFLATION** is the percentage of increase in the prices of all goods and services in the economy.

Inflation also works against investments. In fact, inflation is the enemy of every investment and every investor, because inflation is a function of the economy that essentially makes money worth less over time. There are no investments that are immune to inflation, but some investments fare much better than others. One of your goals as an investor is to figure out which

> **PURCHASING POWER** is the amount of goods or services that money can buy.

investments those are. The rate of return for stocks, for example, has historically more than doubled the rate of inflation.

Let's look at first class postage stamps. In 1974, one stamp cost 10 cents. In 1995, the cost of one stamp jumped to 32 cents. Do you get anything more today for your 32 cents than you did for your 10 cents in 1974? No, you get exactly the same service, or you're supposed to anyway. That's inflation. Inflation has occurred when the same goods or services cost more now than they did in the past.

From here you can go ahead and calculate the "rate of inflation":

$$\textbf{\textit{Rate of Inflation}} = \frac{\textit{Price Today - Price at Start}}{\textit{Price at Start}}$$

For our example with the stamps, that works out to be 220% inflation!

$$\textbf{\textit{Postage Stamp Rate of Inflation}} = \frac{.32 - .10}{.10} = 220\%$$

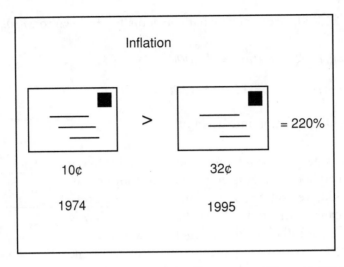

Now don't start writing angry letters to the Postmaster General. This inflation has occurred over a period of twenty years. In fact, the overall inflation rate for the past twenty years is even higher than 220%, so stamp prices are nothing to complain about.

Now let's apply what you know about inflation to our example about savings return. Remember, the rate of return is down to 2.88%, thanks to the IRS. Now you need to add inflation into the mix, but the 220% postage stamp inflation data doesn't help us much here. For one thing, it's only for stamps, and not too many people invest in postage. For another thing, it reflects inflation over a period of twenty years. Since the return is almost always reflected in terms of one-year periods, you want a one-year figure for inflation. You also want a figure for general inflation so you can compare your investment return to the economy overall, not just to stamps. Fortunately, you can find the inflation rate in any good financial periodical such as *The Wall Street Journal* or *Smart Money*.

Let's use the inflation rate for 1992, as shown in the table on the following page, to finish our example. The good news with 1992 is that it had the lowest inflation rate since 1986. The bad news is that you're still losing purchasing power by keeping your money in your savings account! Remember that at the end of the year 1992, you earned 2.88% interest after taxes, but prices rose 3.1% in 1992. That's an effective return of -.22%, which means that at the end of the year, your money, with interest, will buy .22% *less* goods and services than it would have at the beginning of the year. That is a .22% loss in purchasing power. Is this important over the long haul? You bet it is!

20 YEAR INFLATION RATES			
Year	*Inflation*	*Year*	*Inflation*
1976	4.9	1986	1.1
1977	6.7	1987	4.4
1978	9.0	1988	4.4
1979	13.3	1989	4.7
1980	12.5	1990	6.1
1981	8.9	1991	3.7
1982	3.8	1992	3.1
1983	3.8	1993	2.7
1984	4.0	1994	2.8
1985	3.8	1995	3.1

20 Year Average = 5.34%

(Data from Chase Global Data & Research)

$$\textbf{Savings Effective Return} = \textit{Rate of Return - (taxes + inflation)}$$
$$= 4 - (1.12 + 3.1)$$
$$= -.22\%$$

For our $1,000 return, we come up with a loss of $55.

$$\textbf{\$1,000 Effective Return} = \$1,000 - \textit{(taxes + inflation)}$$
$$= \$1,000 - (\$280 + \$775)$$
$$= -\$55$$

Granted, .22% or $55 isn't a staggering loss, but it's still a loss. Remember, we used a relatively low rate of inflation in our example. If you happen to have your money locked up in a long-term CD at 4% and the inflation rate shoots up to somewhere around the 6.1% of 1990, then you're really going to take a bath in terms of purchasing power. Savings accounts and CD's are a great place to keep money for emergencies or short-term needs. However, if you keep *all* your money in savings and CD's, you'll have a very hard time coming up with enough money to meet your financial goals over the long term.

It would be great then if you could take ten simple steps to get wealthy. Unfortunately, no one has that magic formula. Anyone who doesn't want to lose money has to find out the risks before putting money into any investment. I know if I hear that an investment is promising a huge return, the first thing I do is look at the fine print. And I know I'm not alone. Women, in particular, tend be very conservative investors. Again, this all comes from the way women are often discouraged from getting involved. If someone convinces you that something is too difficult for you, it only makes sense that you'd want to avoid it. However, women can turn this conservatism into an advantage as long as it doesn't paralyze them into doing nothing. A healthy skepticism is probably the best way to keep from buying into a "get-rich-quick" scheme that will more often than not land you in the poorhouse.

RISK AND REWARD

The **RISK-RETURN RATIO** is the relationship between an investment's safety and its potential payoff.

There's a very simple rule from real life that applies to just about every investment situation: the higher the risk, the higher the potential return. In financial jargon, this is known as the "risk-return ratio."

Risk and return have a complementary relationship in investing. In simpler terms, that means as risk goes up, so does potential return. When risk comes down, return sinks along with it. That's how the banks get away with offering such low interest rates. If you think about it, you can see that there's no risk at all in a savings account or a CD. That's why you earn such a low interest rate. If the bank gets robbed or fails, the FDIC insurance will pay off depositors. The only way you can possibly lose your money in a bank is if the bank and the government both collapse, but then you've got more problems to worry about than a savings account.

By the way, the lines between banks and brokerage firms are continually blurring today, confusing investors more and more. In the old days, you'd go to the bank to do your banking and to a brokerage firm to buy stocks and bonds. Now you can buy your investments at many banks and do your banking at lots of brokerage firms. The important thing to know is that not everything you buy at a bank is FDIC insured. For example, when you walk into your bank and buy a mutual fund from the person at the investment desk at the end of the lobby, this fund isn't FDIC insured. Many people mistakenly believe that anything they buy at a bank is federally insured, and that simply is not the case. So don't be confused about what is and isn't government guaranteed. When in doubt, ask.

There are, though, plenty of solid, reliable investments out there that offer considerably better returns than savings accounts without exposing you to excessive risk. That's what you're going to learn about in this book. You'll learn to focus on serious long-term investments with significant returns. Once you understand how these investments work and what risks are involved, you'll be able to make informed decisions about your own finances and find investments within your own risk tolerance level that offer you the return you're looking for.

CLASS NOTES

After one class ended, one of the students, Eileen, came up to talk to me. She couldn't get one story out of her mind. "One poor woman," I had told the class, "just came to see me recently. She's 64, and she wants to retire. She worked as an administrative assistant while her husband ran a small retail business that they owned. They'd planned to sell the business and use the money to retire. Unfortunately, her husband died about ten years ago, and she was forced to sell the business. To make matters worse, he didn't have much life insurance.

"So she comes into my office. She only received $30,000 when she sold the business, and she had another $25,000 in two IRA's. Now she works part-time as a sales clerk but wants to retire as soon as possible. I go over the numbers with her, but I know right away she can't make it work. I have to tell this 64-year-old widow that she has to keep her part-time job or change her lifestyle because she can't afford to retire and keep her current standard of living."

Eileen said she shuddered when she thought about it. Her husband, Bill, had died just seven months ago. She was still trying to come to terms with that. And then to hear about a woman in a similar situation who can't afford to retire—it was almost too much for her to handle. She had worked as a secretary for twelve years, never making more than $25,000 a year, and she'd never bothered to participate in her company's retirement plan. Bill always took care of those kinds of things. Bill always took care of everything. From their savings and Bill's life insurance, Eileen had $100,000 in CD's and $20,000 in treasury bills. She said I'd made investing sound great—even *easy—but what if she lost her money? What would she do then? But then what if she didn't do anything and still couldn't afford to retire? She had no idea what to do.*

Her two children were trying to help her plan for her future, but they were each giving her different advice. One told her to keep her money safe in CD's, while the other was pushing mutual funds. Eileen didn't even know what a mutual fund was. But she knew she had to do something. She needed something safe, but she wasn't going to fritter away her money and find out when she was 64 that she couldn't afford to retire.

So, she came to my office. She was still scared to death about losing money on her investments, but she decided she'd rather worry about doing something than worry about doing nothing.

3 Growth *and* INCOME

TYPES OF RETURN

Investments generate return in two ways: growth and income. Income returns are the easiest to understand. Simply put, when your investment earns interest or dividends, you get income. Savings interest is an income return. The bank actually pays you the 4% interest you earn. If you earn a growth return, however, you don't see the money right away. In fact, you don't see any money until you sell your investment. That's because a growth return is an increase in the value of your investment. A simple example of this is a house. If you buy a house for $50,000 and sell it ten years later for $75,000, that $25,000 is the profit from growth. The house ended up being worth $25,000 more than what you paid for it, but you didn't actually get any money until you sold the house.

It's hard to say growth is better than income or income is better than growth, because your investment choices depend on your investment objectives. In the real world of investing, however, growth and income returns are almost never equal. Growth consistently outperforms income in the long term.

> Investment **GROWTH** is an increase in the value of your investment which you do not realize until you sell.

> Investment **INCOME** is tangible money returned to you by your investment.

There are times, such as during retirement, when investors are more likely to want primarily income returns. For the most part, though, when you're looking for long-term investment return, growth returns will outpace income returns.

TYPES OF INVESTMENTS

You can basically do three things with your money to build on what you have.

1. You can keep it in cash or cash equivalents.
2. You can put it in income investments.
3. You can put it in growth investments.

It's important to note that none of these three are mutually exclusive. Some cash equivalents let you earn a little income. Some income investments offer growth. Some growth investments also provide income.

Cash Equivalents

CASH or CASH EQUIVALENTS are cash reserves or anything that can be easily converted into cash.

Cash is the most convenient way to keep your money because you always have ready access to it. Every investor should keep some cash reserves on hand to meet unforeseen emergencies. Both savings accounts and CD's are considered cash equivalents, even though CD's lock your money away for some period of time that you choose. If you need to cash in your CD before it matures, you may pay an early withdrawal penalty. Remember, when you're planning for emergencies, not all cash equivalents are as flexible as cash.

A LIQUID ASSET is cash or an asset you can easily sell for cash without penalty.

Cash and some cash equivalents are also known as liquid assets, which you can always use without penalties.

For example, in a savings account, one dollar always equals one dollar. The value of your principal doesn't change. Don't forget that your purchasing power may be less, but the face value of your money remains the same. Here's a quick illustration: If you have an antique vase that is worth $5,000, the value of that vase is $5,000. But if you can't find someone to buy it right now for $5,000, then your vase is not a liquid asset. $5,000 cash, on the other hand, is always $5,000 cash—completely liquid. Many other investments, including stocks and bonds, are considered very liquid investments, but nothing can be as liquid as simple cash.

In addition to being readily available, cash equivalents generally offer you a return, albeit a rather low return, on your money in the form of interest. Interest is a form of income, because it is a direct payment to you. That means that cash equivalents are generally income investments as well. Therefore, cash and cash equivalents aren't all bad.

Don't forget that there's nothing wrong with keeping *some* of your money in cash equivalents. You need to keep a ready reserve on hand to meet any unforeseen expenses. If, however, you keep all or too much of your money in cash equivalents, you will lose purchasing power and miss out on potential investment opportunities. The toasters and steak knives you get for opening those accounts will be the most expensive household appliances you'll ever buy.

Income Investments

Income investments earn money for their investors. A savings account is probably the easiest—and least profitable—example of an income investment. You know that the bank will pay your interest income on a regular and reliable basis. Bonds that pay regular interest qualify as income investments, as well as all stock dividends. Income investments can increase in value as well, but any investment whose main return is in the form of cash is classified as an income investment.

> INCOME INVESTMENTS generate cash flow.

Income investments generally pay you a fixed rate of return. For example, a bond will pay you 8% interest. That 8% won't change. A fixed rate of return poses an inflation risk for you because if inflation goes up and your return stays the same, your effective return gets smaller. Inflation takes a bigger bite out of your fixed return.

Growth Investments

Growth investments are investments that do not pay you back with a steady stream of income. Instead, the value of your investment increases over time. When you buy a growth investment, you hope for plain and simple price appreciation. If you buy a stock at $10, for example, you would hope to see the price go up to $15, or some similar target. Again, many growth investments are not growth only. Stocks, as in the above example, that rise in value as growth investments, may also pay dividends as income investments.

> A GROWTH INVESTMENT has the potential to increase in value over time.

For the moment, don't think about which investments give you growth, which give you income, and which give you certain combinations of both. All you need to understand here is that there are three basic things you can do with your money:

1. You can keep it in cash or cash equivalents. (Your money does the least work for you there, but it's readily available.)
2. You can choose income investments, which provide you with a steady stream of income.
3. You can opt for growth investments, which don't generate cash flow, but build up value over the long haul.

As an investor, one of your primary goals is to figure out what combination of these three is right for you.

THE CASE FOR GROWTH

Now you've learned that the two biggest enemies of building wealth are taxes and inflation. You also know that you can choose from three basic types of investments: cash, growth, and income.

The one investment category that has consistently and significantly outpaced inflation over the last 20 years is growth. The good news and the bad news about growth is that it's not tied to a fixed return. The stock market never says, "Next year we're going to guarantee you 8%." So, it's *possible* that your return may increase only slightly or even decrease on a very rare occasion. That's the bad news. The good news is that over the long haul, stocks have consistently provided double digit returns.

As you learn more about growth, remember that most of the time it makes sense to balance your portfolio. This means that most of you will want growth, income, *and* cash in your investment portfolio. Certainly, each investor is in a unique financial position that may call for more or less growth vs. income. (Later, you learn how to evaluate your particular financial situation and devise an appropriate portfolio.) Now, you're going to focus solely on growth and why it is important to all investors.

If you are investing for the long term, it is imperative that you look at growth investments and their historically high returns. In addition, since many women tend to be risk averse, very often you're lacking in growth investments.

This brings us back to the impact of inflation and taxes on real return. Naturally, you want to get the highest rate of return possible so that when taxes and inflation take their bite out of your earnings, you're still left with a sizable effective rate of return. You also want to find investments that aren't too risky for your financial situation. To get an idea of what's out there, let's take a look at some rates of return (before taxes and inflation) of some common investments over the last ten and the last twenty years:

	S&P 500	T-bills	Inflation
10-year average	13.94	6.24	3.85
20-year average	13.13	7.66	6.01

(Data from the S&P 500 index, Yields for 91-day Treasury bills, The American Funds Group Research, and Chase Global Data & Research)

The *S&P 500*, short for the *Standard & Poor's 500*, is a stock market indicator that charts the value of 500 stocks. You'll read more about it later, but for now, you need to know that the *S&P 500* gives a good picture of general conditions and broad changes in the stock market based on the average performance of 500 widely held stocks.

T-bills (or Treasury bills, a form of short-term debt issued by the federal government) are income investments.

As you can see, stocks have consistently outperformed T-bills. They don't pay off right away with income, but the growth is substantial. T-bills are steady performers, but they have trouble doing much better than inflation, and we still have to deduct taxes. Another thing you should remember is that these returns are average returns over a long period of time. If you look at short-term, one-year returns, you can find widely varied results. Let's compare 1974 and 1985, for example.

	S&P 500	T-bills	Inflation
1974	-26.4	7.4	12.3
1985	31.1	7.3	3.8

(Data from the S&P 500 index, Yields for 91-day Treasury bills, The American Funds Group Research, and Chase Global Data & Research)

If you owned stocks in 1974, you were crying in your beer, but if you had stocks in 1985, it was time to party. These ups and downs are common in the market, but if you bought the bundle of the *S&P 500* stocks in 1974 and held on to them for twenty years, by 1994 you would have had a 13.13% average annual return, as shown in the 1st table above. Now remember, that's an average. The stock market will have good years and bad years, and that 13.13% average includes not only the big loss in 1974 but also the crash of 1987.

THINKING LONG TERM

You may be thinking that while 1985 looked great for stocks, you would have lost 26.4% of your money if you had stocks in 1974. Why should you put your money in stocks when such wild fluctuations are possible? The key here, and with all growth investing, is to realize that you only lose money if you sell when your investment is down. If you bought in 1974 and sold in 1975, you would have lost money. If you held on for the long term, however, the consistent positive growth returns would have started you on your way to successful investing. Let's go back one more time to why you want to invest—future need and long-term security. And how do you prepare for these goals? You put money aside until you need it. When will you need it? Some time in the future. You want to put money aside and leave it there for a long time, and you want that money to have grown as much as possible when you decide to draw on it. This is thinking long term.

LONG-TERM INVESTING focuses on a return three to five (or more) years down the line.

Thinking long term is the key to successful investing. If you bought the basket of *S&P 500* stocks in 1974, you took a beating. And if you were only looking at the short-term results you probably ran and put your money under the mattress. But if you held on to those same stocks until 1994, your return would have been 1,079%. That works out to a return of $10,790 on an initial investment of $1,000. That means your stock holdings would be worth 11 times what you paid for them. Sure, if you knew the market was declining in 1974, you'd have bought T-bills and then bought stocks right before the market rebounded, but if you knew that, you wouldn't have to worry about investing. You could make millions as an analyst and read fortunes on the side.

Unfortunately, no one knows what the market is going to do. You see all kinds of financial gurus on the news saying the market's going to do this, so buy that, and dump the other. Sometimes they're right, and if you listen to them you could make a lot of money. But guess what? Just as often, they're wrong. Trying to anticipate every move in the economy by constantly shuffling your investments around is the best way to take a beating. You've got to match your investment strategy to your goals. You live for the long term, you need to invest for the long term. Here's an easy rule to remember that will take you a long way if you follow it:

Don't try to time your investments. Give your investments time.

CLASS NOTES

Another student from class, Cindy, also came to see me after taking the class. She was a 28 year-old divorcee with sole custody of her 8-year-old son, Mark. Cindy worked as a customer service representative where she earned $23,000 a year, and she was finishing her degree in computer programming. She also received $150 per month in child support from her ex-husband. Cindy had $500 in savings bonds, $2,000 in a credit union savings account, and was putting 2% of her salary into her company's retirement plan.

Cindy had little experience investing, but she was ready to learn. She was determined that she would be able to pay for her son's education, and she wanted to set the groundwork for expanding her retirement plan and adding some other investments after she completed her degree and landed a better job.

When we first talked, Cindy was somewhat ambivalent about her goals. She was committed to investing the $150 she received every month for her son's education. However, she was reluctant to invest in growth-oriented but more volatile investments. "The numbers look great," she said, "but what if I buy in when the market's high and then it drops? And what if it drops when I'm ready to sell? I can't afford to take chances with Mark's college money."

"You're right to be concerned," I said. "Investments can be volatile. But remember that we're talking long term. Over the long haul, we have seen that stocks and stock mutual funds have consistently outperformed almost all other major investment categories. That doesn't guarantee they're going to keep doing it in the future, but it does make a compelling case for investing in the market. Particularly in a case like yours. You don't need the money for Mark's college for 10 years, so if you're willing to stick it out, history is on your side.

"Sure, over the ten years, your investment will go through some ups and downs, but over the whole ten years, the ups will beat the downs if the market keeps on acting like it has historically."

"But what if I lose money?" Cindy asked.

I explained, "If you don't sell when your investment is down, have you really lost any money?"

"Of course."

"Actually, you haven't," I said. "The value of an investment may fluctuate up and down while you own it, but the only time you gain or lose money is when you sell. You just have to be willing to hold on to it for the long haul."

Cindy started to become convinced. "So over ten years, even if my investment loses money sometimes, it will rebound, and I'll end up making money?"

"Again," I said, "there's no guarantee, but based on the history of the market, you've got a good chance that your money will grow over a ten-year time line."

"And you can help me find growth investments that aren't too volatile?"

"We can find the options that you're most comfortable with. And, we can move into more conservative investments when we get closer to the time Mark needs the money. Then when the time comes, we can use the same kind of strategy to work on your retirement investments."

". . . Because I don't need to get at that money for an even longer time," she said. "Now I'm starting to see it."

4 Stocks

What Is a Stock?

Stocks are the most common and generally most reliable form of growth investment. The caution "generally" applies because there are many volatile stocks that can take you on a ride scarier than any roller coaster. There are also stocks that are income-oriented rather than growth investments, but for now, you should first understand what a stock is and why you should include stocks in your investment portfolio.

> A STOCK is an ownership share of a company.

Simply put, when you own stock in a business, you own part of that business. That's why you may see stocks referred to as equities. In financial lingo, you have an "equity share" of that business. Businesses issue stock to raise money to pay for everything from production and expansion to research and development. In return for your money, businesses give you an ownership share of the company. If the business does well, so do you!

Stock is bought and sold in units called shares. Each share of stock represents one share of ownership. For each share of stock that you own, you are entitled to one vote. If you wish, you may attend the annual meeting and cast your vote there, or you may send a proxy, which casts your vote by mail. These meetings decide everything from the course a business will take to whom will serve as CEO. For large investors and corporations, stock holdings mean control of a business. For the average investor, however, the number of shares held in any individual business probably won't ever amount to more than a token number of votes. You're not likely to ever be able to afford enough shares of IBM stock to take over.

Dividends

A **DIVIDEND** is a portion of a business's profits paid to stockholders.

On the other hand, your ownership stake generally entitles you to share in the profits the business may make. Any payment out of profits is called a dividend.

Not all companies that make money pay dividends to their shareholders. A company's board of directors decides whether the company will pay a dividend and how much each dividend share will be. This is also known as "declaring" a dividend. There are times when companies will choose not to pay any dividends and, instead, put all the profits back in the business to keep it growing. Don't assume that a company which doesn't pay dividends is necessarily a bad investment. Many start-up companies and companies with extensive research expenses, such as biotechnology firms, traditionally reinvest profits rather than declare dividends.

A stock's **TOTAL RETURN** is the increase in stock value (growth) plus any dividend (income) return.

Companies pay dividends in money, shares of stock, or both. The amount and form of any dividend depends on how the business is doing. During good years when the profits have been healthy, dividends tend to go up. In down years when there are few or no profits, dividends may go down or even disappear. Dividends are paid out on a per share basis. For example, if you owned 100 shares of XYZ Corporation stock and the dividend was $1 per share, you would receive $100 in dividends. If, on the other hand, XYZ opted for a stock dividend of 1/10 of a share per share owned, you'd get 10 extra shares of stock to add to your original 100. Dividends are generally paid out quarterly or semi-annually and are the income portion of a stock investment. When you add in stock growth, you can then figure out what is known as the total return on your stocks.

Stock Value

The growth side of a stock investment comes from appreciation in the price of a stock. Essentially, growth is a reflection of how much a buyer is willing to pay for a stock. If buyers like a stock, they bid up the price; if not, they beat it down. Some of the factors that cause stocks to move up and down include the latest line of a company's products, earnings, the type of company and how that sector of the economy is doing, management style, and stability.

Established companies with a good record and proven products, for example, are less likely to suffer serious setbacks or go under than new companies who have nothing to fall back on. Profits, too, obviously make a good benchmark for evaluating a company, particularly future profits. Future profit potential affects a stock's price as much as, if not more than, past performance.

Everyone wants to see a good track record from the company she's investing in. But, you're investing in tomorrow, not in yesterday, and yesterday's best-selling product doesn't guarantee future results. You want to find companies whose products are going to sell tomorrow and whose prospects look good for the future.

There are many sources of information available to you. You'll see many of these companies mentioned in the business sections of newspapers, and most major brokerage firms can provide a list of the stocks they recommend. For more information on a particular topic, read the "Getting Information" section later in this chapter.

Generally, when you invest in a stock, you're hoping that the price of that stock goes up. That way, when it comes time to sell the stock because you're ready to buy a house, send the kids to college, open a business, or retire, you'll be able to get a higher price than what you originally paid for the stock. Consider, for example, XYZ Corporation. If you bought your 100 shares at $10 a piece, your stocks were originally worth $1,000. Subsequently, ten years down the road, the price of XYZ went up to $20 a share. Your same 100 shares are now worth $2,000, but you can only get that extra $1,000 if you sell your stock. Essentially, your $1000 of worth of stock grew to $2,000 worth of stock.

XYZ Growth

	Shares	Price per Share	Value
Today	100	$10	$1000
10 Years Later	100	$20	$2000

10-Year Growth = *value in 10 years - value today = 2000-1000 = $1000*

By now, you're probably thinking this is a pretty optimistic picture—dividends, profits, growth—but what happens when stocks go down? And you're right. Stocks do go down. Prices can fall, and you may lose money if you choose to sell when the current price is less than the price you paid. In the rest of this chapter you're going to learn how to pick quality stocks that should perform well over the long term with little risk of substantial loss.

Of course, when you buy stock, you don't need to calculate how much a stock is worth. The stock market does that for you every day. If you understand what goes into the stock valuation process, however, then you'll have a better understanding of the growth potential and growth mechanism of a stock investment.

Stock Shares

Every company that issues stock issues a certain number of shares. A smaller number of total shares means that each share equals more ownership and a greater slice of the profits pie.

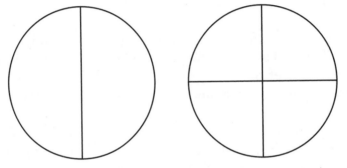

In a really simple example, compare a pie with two slices to a pie with four slices. If you were really hungry (or if the pie were made of profits instead of apples), you'd obviously rather have a piece of the pie with two pieces. The same applies to stocks: the more shares there are, the less significant each individual ownership share becomes. Taken together, stable companies with good future profit potential and a small number of available shares generally command the highest prices for their stocks. Conversely, stocks for new companies which have questionable futures and a large number of shares should cost less.

A **STOCK SPLIT** occurs when the issuing company divides each share of stock into 2 or more shares.

As an investor, your concern shouldn't be how many shares are outstanding, but how your individual shares are going to perform. When stocks rise too much in price, they become less attractive to investors who have to cough up more money to buy into the stock. With that in mind, many companies choose to split their stock when it reaches a high price.

The value of each new share is the value of the old share divided by how many shares it splits into. For example, if your $100 share of XYZ (doing pretty well isn't it?) splits 2 for 1, you end up with two $50 shares for every $100 share you started with. If the $100 share splits 4 for 1, you end up with four $25 shares for each $100 share you started with. Your stock is worth exactly the same amount, you now just have more shares.

Stock Split

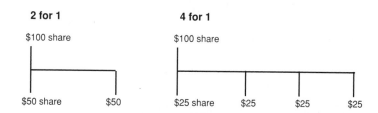

Let's take the example a little further and look at a typical holding of 100 shares at $100 per share. If you own 100 shares of XYZ, when it splits 2 for 1, you end up with 200 shares. If it instead splits 4 for 1, you end up with 400 shares. In every case, the total value of your stock always remains $10,000.

TOTAL VALUE OF XYZ HOLDING

Pre-split: 100 shares worth $100 each = **$10,000** (100 x $100)

2-for-1 split: 200 shares worth $50 each = **$10,000** (200 x $50)

4-for-1 split: 400 shares worth $25 each = **$10,000** (400 x $25)

Whenever a stock splits, the number of shares you own is multiplied by the split, the value of each share is divided by the split, and the total value of the shares you own stays the same.

Stock splits are initiated by the issuing company and voted on at the stockholders meetings. Once a split is agreed upon, all shares are split. You don't get to decide whether you want your share to split or not. Each new split share gives you one vote and one dividend claim, but the value of your total votes and dividend claims remains the same because the total number of shares has increased by the same factor as your individual shares.

XYZ Votes

	Your shares	*Total Shares*	*% of Votes*
Pre-split:	100 shares	100,000 shares	**.1%** (100/100,000)
2-for-1 split:	200 shares	200,000 shares	**.1%** (200/200,000)
4-for-1 split:	400 shares	400,000 shares	**.1%** (400/400,000)

1 Share = 1 Vote

XYZ Dividends

Pre-split: 100 shares paying $1 each = **$100** (100 x $1)

2-for-1 split: 200 shares paying $.50 each = **$100** (200 x $.50)

4-for-1 split: 400 shares paying $.25 each = **$100** (400 x $.25)

By lowering the per share price, your stock becomes more attractive to new investors which, in turn, frequently drives the price back up.

A **Reverse Stock Split** occurs when a company combines a certain number of shares into one, higher priced share.

Similarly, if a company feels that it's stock price has fallen too low, which could also deter investors, it might choose to implement a reverse split.

For example, if XYZ had a reverse split 2 to 1 when XYZ stock sold for $10, a 100-share holding at $10 per share before the reverse split would become a 50-share holding at $20 per share after the reverse split. Again, the total value of your stock remains the same.

How the Stock Market Works

Stocks are bought and sold in two ways: in a stock exchange or "over the counter." A stock exchange is a formal setting where stock transactions, also called trading, occur. There are a number of stock exchanges in the U.S., ranging from the huge New York Stock Exchange, the largest and busiest stock exchange in the world, to regional stock exchanges with far smaller trading volume.

You can visit a stock exchange if you want to see where it all happens. In fact, the pandemonium and frenzy of the New York Stock Exchange makes it one of the most popular tourist attractions in New York City.

A stock exchange is governed by strict rules which not only regulate trading but also determine which stocks may be traded at a given exchange. Over the counter (or OTC) trading, on the other hand, is stock trading that occurs outside a formal stock exchange. Over the counter trading takes place over computer networks and is also regulated by the government. Traditionally, OTC stocks have been issued by smaller companies who couldn't meet listing requirements of the New York Stock Exchange, such as annual net income, number of shares outstanding, and value of shares. Recently however, many successful companies that can meet these requirements are choosing to remain OTC, including many of the technology companies like Microsoft and Intel.

Market Trends

All stock markets experience periods when stock prices go up and periods when stock prices decline. These trends tend to match the state of the economy, but shocks of all sorts, from political to ecological, can swing the market from one extreme to the other. For now, you'll look at the two major market swings, up and down, because they affect everything from what kind of stock you buy, to when you buy it and when you sell it.

> A **BULL MARKET** is a market where stock prices are generally going up.

Bull and bear markets are terms that stock analysts and economists love to throw around. The terms are important because they help us figure out what the market is doing by pointing out the current direction of the market. When an analyst declares a bull market, the analyst is saying that he or she believes the market will continue to rise for some time. A bear market, by contrast, seems poised to continue dropping. The key to remember here, of course, is that these analysts are, in fact, wrong some of the time. The terms are used often enough, though, that every investor ought to know what they mean.

> A **BEAR MARKET** is market where stock prices are generally going down.

Buying and Selling Stock

Buying and selling stock is different from buying and selling just about anything else. You can't go down to the mall and buy shares of AT&T, and you can't advertise your stock shares in the newspaper with the garage sale ads. Stock trades are almost always executed by a licensed professional. You'll learn about the types and fees of brokers later, but first you should understand the mechanics of stock trades.

If you've ever looked at the stock page in the newspaper, you've probably noticed that you don't see any dollar signs, but you do see lots of fractions. This looks very arcane and confusing, but it's really very simple. All stocks are listed, bought, and sold in terms

A POINT is a measure of a stock's value that equals $1.

of dollars. Fractions in the price listing equal cents. A stock that lists at 25 1/4 is worth $25.25. A stock that goes up 1/2 has increased 50¢ in value. The most common fractions you'll see on the stock page are halves, quarters, and eighths, but stocks can trade in sixteenths, thirty-seconds, and even sixty-fourths. Crunching those fractions can get a little messy, but it's still easier than working in increments of 1¢. By standardizing stock prices in fractions rather than pennies, dealing in fractions keeps trading from degenerating into a battle of pennies and makes record keeping a lot easier.

Sometimes you might see stock prices referred to in terms of points. One point equals one dollar with stocks. (When you're dealing with bonds, points mean something entirely different.)

A ROUND LOT is 100 shares of stock or any multiple of 100 (*e.g.*, 100, 200, 300, *etc.*).

You can buy stocks in round and odd lots—multiples of 100 shares, or numbers less than 100, respectively. For example, 52 shares would be an odd lot. 108 shares would be considered one round lot of 100 shares and one odd lot of 8 shares. Most stock transactions involve round lots, and the buy and sell mechanisms of the markets are designed to handle round lots of 100 shares of stock. In fact, you may even have to pay a higher commission to your broker to buy or sell odd lots of stock, because your broker can't use normal market procedures. Therefore, as an investor, you're better off buying stocks in round lots if you can.

An ODD LOT is any number of stock shares less than 100.

When you want to buy a stock, call your broker and tell him or her what stock and how many shares you want to purchase. Once you've told your broker what stock and how many shares you want to buy, he or she will tell you the market price of the stock you're interested in.

The MARKET PRICE is the current selling price of stock.

Let's go back to XYZ Corporation to illustrate this transaction. Suppose you told your broker that you wanted to buy 100 shares of XYZ—one round lot. Your broker checks the latest information on XYZ and says, "XYZ is trading at 24 3/4 by 25 1/4." This means that the current trading price to buy is 25 3/4, and the current price to sell is 25 1/4. The high number is what you would pay to buy XYZ stock. The low number is the price you would get if you sold XYZ shares. The price difference is the spread which includes profit for the traders. That does not include the commission you'll pay your broker on the transaction.

If you think $25.25 is a pretty fair price for XYZ, you tell your broker to go ahead and buy 100 shares at the market price. When you tell your broker to buy at the market price, you're telling him or her to buy your stock right away at the prevailing price. Now, it's still possible that you might end up paying a little less, or even a little more, than $25.25 for XYZ in this case. The market price for XYZ one minute might not be the market price in the next minute. When your broker gets your order, he or she will enter the trade, which tells the traders to buy 100 shares of XYZ for you at the best price currently available. That price will be somewhere around $25.25, but you won't know the exact price until the traders actually buy the stock. Here's how the buying process works.

For most long-term investors, and that's what you always have to remember that you are, buying at the market price is usually the best route. When you're in a stock for the long haul, a 1/4 point here or there doesn't make that much difference to your overall investment success. Just about every investor, however, will come across some stock that he or she would like to buy, but will want to wait and see what's going to happen first. You might want to try to make sure a stock has stopped falling in price before you buy it. That's never a bad idea. Or you might want to make sure a stock you heard about is really on the way up before you jump on the bandwagon. Remember, brokers are flexible, and they can trade stocks in many ways to meet your specific requirements.

Let's get back to your XYZ order. Remember, you told your broker to go ahead and buy 100 shares at the market price when it was 25 1/4. After your broker enters your order, one of two things will happen. If the stock you want to buy is traded at an exchange, the traders will buy your stock on the trading floor. If the stock you want to buy is traded over the counter, the whole transaction is done electronically via computer networks, but the process is essentially the same in both cases. Traders for buyers and sellers haggle over a sale price using strict guidelines and reach agreements which are constantly reported.

When you want to buy at the market price, the trader who receives your order will try to buy your stock at the best price available. Traders always try to get the best deals for their clients because they want to keep them as clients. If your broker told you the market price was $25.25 a share, but the trader ended up paying $30.00 a share, you'd obviously be pretty unhappy. Your trader knows this and will seek out other traders willing to sell for a price right around the market price you were quoted. When your trader feels he or she has found a seller offering the best price, the two traders will then agree on the transaction.

Everything works the same way if you want to sell. If you call your broker with instructions to sell your 100 shares of XYZ at the market price, he or she will pass your order along to the trader in the same way. This time though, your trader will be the one looking for a buyer, but again, your trader will try to land you the best possible price.

One final thing to note is that virtually every time you make a stock trade, you're going to have to pay some kind of commission. Again, the type and amount of commission will vary with the kind of broker you use, but let's look at a simple example to help illustrate this point.

Suppose the market price for XYZ is $15 a share when you buy 100 shares. You then hold on to your 100 shares until the price goes up to $25 a share, at which point you decide to sell. XYZ rose from $15 a share when you bought, to $25 a share when you sold. That means you ended up making $10 a share, right? Wrong! You need to factor in the broker's commission for every transaction. With that included, you actually end up paying more than $15 for every share of XYZ you buy, and you get less than $25 for every share of XYZ you sell. Let's look at how this plays out using estimated commissions.

BUYING AND SELLING 100 SHARES OF XYZ

Original Purchase	*Selling Your Shares*	*Your Bottom Line* *(sale price – purchase price)*
If trading were free:		
100 shares @ $15 = **$1500**	100 shares @ $25 = **$2500**	$2500-$1500 = **$1000**
In the real world:		
100 shares @ $15 + $52 commission = **$1552**	100 shares @ $25 – $72 commission = **$2428**	$2428-$1552 = **$876**

The moral of the commission story is, "Don't buy and sell lightly." Buying and selling stock costs you money in the form of commissions, so make sure you're ready to buy or you really want to sell before you call your broker with the order.

These basic principles of stock trading are the same for both stock exchanges and the over the counter market. Each handles the specifics of trading a little differently, though.

Stock Exchanges

In a stock exchange (*not* the OTC), traders meet face to face to buy and sell stocks on the trading floor. Any time a trader wants to buy or sell a certain stock, XYZ for example, he or she goes over to where XYZ is traded and deals with other traders who have come to trade XYZ stock. If the trader's next order is to buy QRS stock, he or she would have to walk, in theory, or sprint, if you've ever seen a real stock exchange, over to where QRS stock trades. In essence, a stock market is like any other market where buyers and sellers get together to haggle over prices. It's just that with a stock market, the traders are haggling over millions of dollars rather than a few cents per pound for grapes.

U.S. Stock Exchanges		
American	*Intermountain*	*Pacific*
Boston	*Midwest*	*Philadelphia*
Cincinnati	*New York*	*Spokane*

"Over the Counter" Trading (NASDAQ)

The "over the counter" stock market in the U.S. is also known as NASDAQ, short for the National Association of Security Dealers Automated Quotation System.

NASDAQ is the national, computer-based "over the counter" stock market.

NASDAQ is a complex computer network that allows over the counter traders to interact with each other and conduct stock trades without being in the same physical location. In the U.S. stock market, the terms "NASDAQ" and "over the counter" can be used interchangeably. It used to be that NASDAQ was the place where start-up companies would earn their stripes as reliable companies. Nowadays, though, many large and successful corporations trade their stock on the NASDAQ. The current list of NASDAQ stocks includes Apple Computers, Intel, MCI, and Coors, just to name a few.

The New York Stock Exchange, the American Stock Exchange, NASDAQ, and all the other exchanges like to tout themselves as special and better places to put your money. For all investors, though, it really doesn't matter what market a stock trades in. You're investing in stock, and that means you're investing in a company, not a market. Therefore, your main concern has to be which stock you want to buy.

TYPES OF STOCKS

Now that you understand the basics of stocks, you can start to learn about some key nuts and bolts issues of investing. As you read this chapter, it is important to remember that the details about stocks apply to both the stock market *and* stock mutual funds. For example, the definitions of growth and income stocks will come in handy when you see the types of stocks that various mutual funds buy. The same holds true for the other key points such as thinking long term, buying stocks on sale, and evaluating risk and return.

Stocks can be divided and grouped in a variety of ways from industry to size to geographic location. All those endless distinctions do is obscure the decision-making process by diverting your focus from what should be the critical question: "Will these stocks get me the return I'm looking for, and am I comfortable with the risks involved?" First, though, you should understand a few classifications of stocks that you're likely to come across and that *are* important to consider when making investment decisions.

Common Stock Vs. Preferred Stock

COMMON STOCK is an ownership share in a company that gives you one vote on the selection of directors and other important matters, and dividends if they are paid.

Common and preferred stocks are the two main types of stock shares you can buy. They are listed, in fact, as common and preferred in the stock markets. When you buy shares of stocks, your trade confirmation statement will say either common or preferred on it. When most people, including financial advisors, refer to stocks, though, they are talking about common stocks.

Common stocks make up the vast majority of stock issues traded on the major markets. Common stocks generally experience more growth (and decline) than preferred stocks. As voting shares, common stocks offer the investor more of a role in a company's operations. However, dividends are paid to common stocks after all dividends are paid to preferred stocks, and only if sufficient profits remain to pay out more dividends. To sum all that up, with common stock you ride along with the successes and failures of a company more than you do with preferred stock. One way to look at the two types is that you buy common stocks for growth and preferred stocks for income.

Preferred stock, in fact, performs almost more like a bond than a stock. You'll read more about bonds in chapter 5, but for now just know that preferred stock generates more income than growth. In addition to having first claim on dividends, preferred stock may also have a guaranteed dividend that must be paid even if the company loses money. In any case, the dividend from preferred stock is usually much higher than from common stock. Furthermore, most preferred stocks do not come with voting privileges. Taken together, that means that you generally buy your preferred stock and wait for the dividends to roll in. Being more stable than common stock, preferred stock growth potential is generally less, classifying the high dividend preferred stock as an income stock.

PREFERRED STOCK is an ownership share in a company generally without voting rights but with preference over common stock dividends.

The Risk and Return Spectrum

There are literally thousands and thousands of stocks in the financial universe with many dramatically different risk and return characteristics. Different stocks generate different returns and should be purchased for different investment goals. Stocks simply don't fit neatly into categories. They fit into a stock spectrum ranging from pure growth to pure income. Unless you understand these distinctions, you can buy the wrong stock and never understand why it isn't behaving as you think it should.

Now, you'll learn in detail about a few stock categories and their characteristics so that you will be better able to buy the stocks that fit your risk tolerance and investment goals. This is easiest to see with a couple of diagrams:

Stock Spectrum

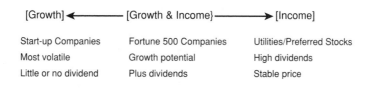

[Growth] ◄——— [Growth & Income} ———► [Income]

Start-up Companies	Fortune 500 Companies	Utilities/Preferred Stocks
Most volatile	Growth potential	High dividends
Little or no dividend	Plus dividends	Stable price

**Potential Stock Risk
(Volatility)**

Growth   Growth & Income   Income

Growth Stocks

GROWTH STOCKS are riskier than average stocks, have high P/E ratios, and pay little or no dividend, but have the potential for appreciation in price.

Growth stocks are issued by companies who may have little or no track record; therefore, their stocks could go way up or way down. When you buy growth stocks you are investing wholly in a company's potential. You're hoping that the company will take off and the price of the stock will increase considerably. You're not expecting dividends, but you really don't care, because you know that potential equals growth. Dividends come from profits, and new companies aren't likely to realize much initial profit. Even if these companies do make some early profits, these companies are more likely to reinvest the money in the business than pay a dividend.

P/E RATIO (Price/Earnings Ratio) is the ratio of the current market price of a stock divided by its Earnings Per Share (the amount of profit allocated to each share). For example, a stock with a market price of $70 and an earnings per share of $1 would have a P/E ratio of 70.

If the potential you're banking on pans out, however, you could wind up laughing all the way to the bank. You could even start to see some dividends. If, though, your sure thing ends up a bust, so does your investment. The risk-reward relationship is the key consideration with "pure" growth stocks. High potential gain always goes hand-in-hand with big potential loss.

The moral of the growth stock story is if you're the kind of investor who would throw yourself in front of a bus if your account value ever drops, you are probably not a good candidate for growth stocks (or growth mutual funds).

Growth & Income Stocks

GROWTH & INCOME STOCKS are stocks with potential for both price increase and dividends.

Most people don't want a wild ride with investments. That's why most investors focus more on middle-of-the-road, growth & income stocks. Growth & income stocks are generally issued by established companies with a good history of profits and reliability. These companies' stocks aren't likely to shoot through the roof, but they're not likely to fall through the floor either. Growth & income stocks reflect the stability and the profitability of the company that issues them and generate a good total return. You should expect moderate growth as the company continues to do well, and you should expect a dividend from the steady stream of profits that the company generates.

Stocks from Fortune 500 companies and the companies that make up the *Standard & Poor's 500* are good examples of stocks that would be called growth & income stocks. The *S&P 500* stocks, you will recall, averaged a 13.13% average annual return during the twenty years from 1974 to 1994, and at the end of 1995, the return was 14.53%. (That's an increase in price, so that means growth.) These stocks frequently have annual dividend yields of over 2%. Admittedly, that's nothing to write home about, but remember that's in addition to the growth return.

Income Stocks

Investors that want a steady income flow from their stocks look to income-oriented stocks to meet their needs. Income stocks come from companies with a steady profit stream that aren't likely to experience either major expansion or major setbacks. Utility company stocks are the quintessential examples of income stocks. They're stable; they're always going to be there, and they'll always have a steady stream of income. Income stocks reflect the stability of those sorts of companies.

> **INCOME STOCKS** are low volatility common stocks that are likely to pay high dividends.

They pay out a high dividend, frequently in excess of 5%, and typically don't experience huge price swings. That means with an income stock, you're even less likely to have price volatility than with a growth & income stock. You're also less likely to see any huge increase in the price of your stock. You're essentially sacrificing some growth for stability and income.

With all this focus on growth, growth, and more growth, you may assume that income stocks are bad. However, income investments are an important part of virtually every portfolio. Investing in income stocks can be a very safe way to earn a high rate of income and still see some appreciation in the price of the stock. Your return won't generally be as great as the growth return on a growth & income stock, but your risk is less, too. (Always remember risk and reward.) Furthermore, even though you're giving up growth for income, the price of an income stock will still generally move up over the long haul and give you some growth.

Let's look at an example of an income stock to further clarify the picture. Public Service Company of Colorado is the major gas and electric company in Colorado, which places them in a pretty solid position. No matter what's going on in the economy, people need heat and lights. There's really no alternative available (to most residents). They're going to keep pulling in profits every year from the same two products—gas and electricity.

Public Service Company stock, therefore, performs like the classic income stock. The price of the stock is relatively stable, and each share pays out dividends that average around 5.8% at today's price. Although, even these relatively safe growth stocks can experience some volatility. Utilities like Public Service Company, for example, move up and down with interest rates. Over the long haul, however, their general stability and high dividends have proven utilities to be good income investments.

Defensive and Cyclical Stocks

DEFENSIVE STOCKS are stocks that remain relatively unaffected by changes in the economy. These stocks are often referred to as "well-defended."

There are two more important definitions that you need to know before you try to make your fortune buying stocks: defensive and cyclical stocks. You need to understand these kinds of stocks not so you can try to time the market, but so you will understand how the stocks you buy will perform during different economic times. Not all stocks fit in these two categories, but many do, and you will certainly see and hear these terms as you read about stocks in the newspaper.

What does "well-defended" mean? It means that defensive stocks represent companies whose products you buy no matter what the economic conditions are. You buy these products regardless of whether interest rates are high or low, inflation is high or low, or the country is in a recession. These stocks tend to be relatively unaffected by these economic conditions, hence the name, "defensive." The simplest way to understand defensive stocks is to consider what you would buy no matter what the economic conditions are.

When I ask that question in my class, the most common and correct response I get is food. No matter how tough times get, people buy food. Beverage stocks typically go in concert with food, so they too have historically been defensive. Although this is how most of us would respond, one student eagerly gave the answer "toilet paper." That never occurred to me, but it shows that not everybody has the same idea of what they can't do without. Other common examples of defensive stocks include some drug companies and utilities because people also tend to take their medicine, as well as heat and light their homes, in any economic climate.

CYCLICAL STOCKS are stocks whose prices are affected by changes in the economic cycle.

As you may have suspected, cyclical stocks are the exact opposites of defensive stocks. Cyclical stocks are the kind of stocks that fluctuate a great deal with changes in interest rates, inflation rates, and other economic factors. If a defensive stock represents goods you'd buy no matter what, a cyclical stock comes from a company whose products you would delay buying if interest rates were too high or you were worried about losing your job. Companies whose stocks are cyclical sell products people put off buying during tough times. Obvious examples include housing, appliances, heavy equipment, cars, and luxury items.

If you own cyclical stocks, you need to be aware that just because these companies' products aren't currently selling well, that doesn't mean that demand has gone away. Demand does *not* go away, it gets pent up so that as economic conditions improve, these products suddenly return to high demand. For example, if you need a new car, you need a new car. If the economy looks bleak, you simply delay your purchase until economic conditions improve and you feel you can afford it.

The experience of Peoria, Illinois–based Caterpillar over the last few years is a good example of what I mean by a cyclical stock. Caterpillar, an established company that makes tractors and construction vehicles, is one of the *Dow Jones 30 Industrial* stocks. They do a steady business, but a business that falls off in recessions when fewer construction projects start up and companies try to make their old equipment last a little longer. In 1992, when the economy was down, Caterpillar stock sank to near $40 a share. It recently split 2 for 1 at a little over $113 a share. There's more to that explosion in price than simple economic cycles, but that gives you an idea of what can happen to a stock that traditionally moves with the economy. By the way, for those of you who are sure I made a killing on Caterpillar, I didn't. That's one I missed out on. The really sad part about this one is that I'm from Peoria, Illinois too.

INVESTING IN STOCKS

The first thing you always need to remember about the stock market is the risk-reward ratio. Stocks run the whole gamut from low risk–low return through moderate risk–steady return to huge risk–anybody's guess what it will return. In the financial world these stocks are labeled according to their volatility.

VOLATILITY measures how risky a stock is.

You can buy more conservative stocks (low volatility) that will pay you a steady dividend. You can buy moderate stocks (moderate volatility) that may also pay you a steady dividend and will rise and fall with the market and the economy. You can buy riskier stocks (high volatility) that could hit the big time or go belly up before you can pick up the phone to tell your broker to sell. The key to sorting through all these choices and making money in the stock market is understanding the risks and rewards involved and buying the kinds of stocks that fit your personal risk tolerance.

Beating the Risk

Some investors fail. It's inevitable, but it's frequently avoidable. Chances are you will fail if you always try to outguess the market. If you play it smart and stick with the long-term perspective, you'll greatly increase your chances for success. You won't get rich quick, but you will find quality, long-term investments that will pay off over time if you . . .

Think Long Term

It's worth repeating:

> *To be a successful investor in the stock market, you have to think long term.*

If you want to get rich quick, you might as well go to Vegas and play the slots. None of the get rich schemes I've heard of are any more reliable than that. If, though, you want a reliable, long-term investment that will outperform taxes and inflation—and that should always be your goal—the stock market may be a great place to invest your money. There is, of course, no iron-clad guarantee you will make money in the stock market. The stock market (as we've seen with the *S&P 500*) has produced good, long-term results, but again, there's no guarantee of future success.

Obviously, not every stock is going to be a great investment. Businesses fold all the time, and sure things turn into the next Edsel more often than the next IBM. You can take steps to protect yourself from too much volatility, though. If you invest in stocks issued by quality companies and hold on to them, you will get quality results over the long term. By quality companies, I'm referring to Fortune 500 companies, companies with household names that have been around for years, and the like.

Let's take a detailed look at the return on the *S&P 500* over the last twenty years. The *S&P 500* makes a good yardstick because the stocks it tracks come from established, "quality" companies with large numbers of investors.

Let's focus first on the average return figures. Over those 20 years, the stocks that make up the *S&P 500* performed better than long-term bonds and T-bills, and they significantly outpaced inflation. If you examine strictly those average return numbers, the stock market looks pretty appealing. Not too many investors are going to turn down an average annual return of better than 14.5% every year for twenty years. That's an excellent return, and that's exactly what you should be looking for in an investment—

20 YEAR INVESTMENT RETURNS, 1975–1994

Year	S&P 500	Bonds	T-bills	Inflation
1976	23.6	15.6	4.5	4.9
1977	-7.4	3.0	6.3	6.7
1978	6.4	1.2	9.4	9.0
1979	18.2	2.3	12.6	13.3
1980	32.3	3.1	16.4	12.5
1981	-5.0	7.3	11.3	8.9
1982	21.9	31.1	8.2	3.8
1983	22.4	8.0	9.3	3.8
1984	6.1	15.0	8.3	4.0
1985	31.1	21.3	7.3	3.8
1986	18.6	15.6	5.7	1.1
1987	5.1	2.3	5.9	4.4
1988	16.8	7.6	8.4	4.4
1989	31.4	14.2	7.9	4.7
1990	-3.3	8.3	7.0	6.1
1991	16.0	12.8	5.9	3.7
1992	7.6	8.5	3.4	3.1
1993	10.1	12.2	3.0	2.7
1994	1.3	1.3	5.0	2.8
1995	37.5	21.0	5.6	3.1
20-year average	14.53	10.59	7.57	5.34
Last 10-year avg.	14.11	10.38	5.78	3.61

(Data from the S&P 500 index, the Lehman Brothers Bond Index, Yields for 91-day Treasury bills, Chase Investment Performance Digest, and Chase Global Data & Research)

a stable, long-term return that beats inflation. Remember, the 14.5% figure is an average. If you don't always keep that in mind, the short-term ups and downs we talked about will drive you crazy, especially the downs.

Don't Buy High and Sell Low

Unfortunately, the stock market does its best to scare investors away before there's any long-term return. Everyone knows that the stock market moves up and down, and anyone who's ever owned stock can tell you that the market may take your stock on a bumpy ride with it. Remember the 1974 return from chapter 3? A -26.4% return is a scary number. If you had your money in the *S&P 500* in 1974, every $100 at the beginning of the year was only worth $74.60 by the end of year. If I sold you stocks in 1974 and you lost 26.4% that year alone, you'd want to string me up. Hopefully for me though, while you were tying the knot for the noose, I'd be able to distract you with the average return figures. That 13.13% return over 20 years *includes* the -26.4% of 1974.

If you decided at the end of 1974 to cut your losses and get out of this crazy stock market, you'd be pretty miserable. If, however, you overcame your fear and trusted in the long term, by the end of 1993, each $100 of stock you bought at the end of 1973 would be worth $1153.31 (if you add up all the returns). That's what steady, long-term growth can do for you.

Unfortunately, to get that long-term growth, you'd have to go against your natural instincts and hold on to your stock even when the market drops. In fact, the most common mistake the average investor makes is buying high, selling low, and wondering what went wrong. In the financial world, this is known as the "whipsaw" effect, because you get slashed at both ends. To beat the whipsaw, you've got to remember to invest with your head and not your gut, and to always think long term.

This isn't to say that you ought to hold on to every loser stock until it drags you down in flames. A large part of investing in stocks is knowing when to get out, which means knowing when your stock isn't just experiencing a temporary lull but is really taking a bath. You'll learn more about this when you read about managing your stocks later in this chapter. The key is to not buy and sell stocks on a whim. You should be thoroughly convinced that you have a good reason before you sell. If you sell your stock every time it goes down, you'll never hold on to anything long enough to see any long-term return. You'll also be lining some stockbroker's pockets since each time you buy or sell a stock you have to pay a commission. Bear in mind the following phrase which will serve you well in the stock market:

> *Investors make themselves money. Traders frequently make their brokers money.*

Buy Stocks "On Sale"

If this were a perfect world, and all wishes came true, the stock market would do nothing but go up forever. Well, the world isn't perfect, and the stock market obeys the law of gravity like everything else. What goes up must come down. The stock market has its bumps up and down with its highs and lows. Since you'll have to accept the fact that there are market declines, you should know what they mean in terms of your investment portfolio.

When the stock market goes down, I tell my classes to consider it a time when stocks are "on sale." Let's think about that for a minute. I, along with many of my friends, love sales. My friends kid me that when I see a sale sign I go over, pick up the item, buy it, and *then* ask, "What is it?" What does it mean for something to be on sale? The obvious answer is when it's marked down. But, when are you least likely to buy stocks or stock mutual funds? You got it, when they are marked down.

It's fascinating to see that this is one area where women truly don't like sales. In fact, when the market goes on sale, we're more apt to sell than to buy. This is a good example of how following your gut can be the wrong thing.

Since the market has recovered time after time to reach new historical highs, all of the previous pullbacks have been wonderful buying opportunities. This doesn't guarantee that all future pullbacks will offer the same great bargains, but it's a heck of a convincing upward trend line. Frequently, when stocks are down, you should be buying. Many times my clients have come back and said that by remembering that concept—that things are on sale when they are marked down, and stocks are no exception—they are able to stick it out or even add to their positions during tough times in the market.

Think of it this way: Suppose you wanted to buy a car, and you saw it advertised in the paper for $10,000. Now suppose you went to look at that car, and the owner said he decided he only wanted $8,000. Would you be apt to tell him, "You can't fool me, I'm going to wait until you mark it up to the full $10,000 before I buy it?" Sounds crazy doesn't it? And you'd never do it. But this is exactly what people often do with stocks and stock mutual funds when the market goes down. If you follow some of the basic rules—buy quality and hold it, and always remember that you may have to go against your gut—you will be positioning yourself well for long-term gains.

Buying Stocks

Hopefully, by now, you're starting to think that this stock "thing" sounds pretty inviting. After all, it seems that you can make a lot of money in stocks. Still, the worst thing you can do with stocks, like any investment, is rush out and buy the first stock you come across without knowing anything about it or what your alternatives are. When you've decided that you want to take advantage of the potential returns from the stock market, you need to do some preliminary investigation. You need to find out what stocks look good for the future, what stocks have proven themselves in the past, and what stocks match your own investment goals and risk tolerances. To start this process, you need to find out where you can learn these things.

Getting Information

VALUE LINE and *STANDARD & POOR'S* are independent stock rating services.

There are many ways you can get data on stocks: newspapers, financial publications, other media, research materials from brokerage firms, etc. Two of the most respected sources for information on stocks are *Value Line* and *Standard & Poor's*.

Both *Value Line* and *Standard & Poor's* give in-depth reports and detailed analyses of many stocks that trade in U.S. markets. These reports cover everything from the stock's performance history to the stability and profit potential of the company that issued the stock. *Value Line* also gives you future target price ranges for each stock. You won't find those projections in *Standard & Poor's,* but *S&P* does provide a lot of information about each company.

Both publications have guides that explain how you can best use the information that they provide. In the *Value Line*, for instance, you will find information relating to current price, P/E ratio, target price projections, and ratings for timeliness (relative price performance for the next 12 months) and safety (credit quality of the company). At the bottom of each page, you'll find a user-friendly analysis of key events and future prospects for the company being reviewed. *Standard & Poor's* stock reports provide much of the same information in a different format, without target price projections. Instead, they provide a stock outlook ranking on a scale of 1 to 5, 5 being the highest.

You can find these two publications at many local libraries. When you start to use these reference guides, you'll notice that many of the well-known companies such as Taco Bell, Burger King, and Target department stores aren't listed because they are owned by other companies. That means you can't buy stock in Burger King, but you can buy stock in Burger King's parent company, Grand Metropolitan, a British company whose stock trades on the New York Stock Exchange. If you do buy stock in a company like Grand Metropolitan, for example, your stock then represents ownership of every company Grand Metropolitan owns. In Grand Metropolitan's case, that list includes Pillsbury, Jolly Green Giant, Häagen-Dazs, Pearl Vision Centers, Alpo, and many major liquor labels.

Unfortunately, neither *Value Line* nor *Standard & Poor's* give a list of what companies own what other companies. To find that information, you have to turn to *Who Owns Who in America*, another publication you can find at your library.

Who Owns Who in America lists companies that own or are owned by other companies.

In *Who Owns Who in America* you can find up-to-date information on who owns what. So, if you're sure Taco Bell is the next big thing, you'll be able to find out that you'll need to buy stock in PepsiCo to share in the wealth.

With *Value Line, Standard & Poor's,* and *Who Owns Who in America,* you can track down information on many companies that you might want to invest in whose stock trades in the U.S., although you may have a hard time finding information about stock from small companies. In any case, you'll quickly find that if you simply pick up any of these publications and start going through it company by company, you'll get hopelessly bogged down in the vast amount of information you encounter. To make sense of this information, you have to know how to use it.

Evaluating Risk & Return

Unless you want to spend your whole life reading through *Value Line* or *Standard & Poor's,* you should narrow down the prospective stocks you want to consider buying before you start your research. You might have a good feeling about a couple of companies, or you might have read about some good investment bets. There's certainly no shortage of financial magazines, newspapers, and columns that are only too happy to give advice on the next hot stock. However, as with any so-called "expert advice," you need to take this information with a grain of salt and do your own homework. Financial publications can serve as a good starting point by suggesting some stocks for you to look into, and you may want to take a look at what either *Value Line* or *Standard & Poor's* has to say about a company before investing in it.

When you start researching stocks from most large companies, you'll find that it isn't difficult to find data. In fact, there's almost too much out there. For example, nearly every major stock brokerage firm provides a list of recommended stocks that their analysts compile. These lists frequently rank stocks either "buy," "sell," or "hold." In addition, many major companies have investor relations departments that will send you all manner of information about their particular company and its stock. Many of these firms even have toll free numbers and are more than happy to provide information on the wonders of their stock.

Buying Quality Stocks

Obviously, you want this time spent on getting accurate and complete information to pay off. The aim of your research efforts should always be to find quality stocks, usually those of established companies with long track records of solid products and earnings.

When you pick up a *Value Line,* look for stocks with high safety and financial strength ratings, and be sure to check out the long-term projections. If *Standard & Poor's* is more your style, pay close attention to the *S&P* rating. Keep in mind, though, that despite the excellent information in both *Standard & Poor's* and *Value Line,* there are no guarantees that stocks will perform as expected. Don't make your decisions based solely on information from these two sources. There are lots of other resources out there. Remember, too, that you're in this for the long-term pay-off, and over the long haul it's the quality stocks that tend to pay the reliable returns.

Diversify, Diversify, Diversify

BLUE CHIP refers to the common stock of a nationally known company that has a long history of being profitable and paying dividends. Blue chip stocks are frequently high-priced and enjoy a good reputation, for example, IBM, AT&T, and General Motors.

No matter how high the quality of the stock you buy—even if it's the bluest of the blue chips—there is no guarantee that it won't hit some turbulent waters. Even the best of companies can suffer an unexpected setback or disaster that can send its stock price plummeting. That's why every smart investor spreads her investments around. This is known as diversifying your portfolio.

To properly diversify your investment portfolio, you need to put assets in different investment categories: stocks, bonds, and money markets, for example. Suppose you put every penny of your investment money in Disney and then a hurricane wiped out Disneyland or an earthquake swallowed up Disneyworld and Disney's movie studios. What do you think would happen to the price of Disney stock? What do you think would happen to your investment?

DIVERSIFYING means spreading your assets between different investments or different investment categories.

Nature carrying out a vendetta against Mickey Mouse might seem a little far-fetched, but suppose the only stock you owned was 1,000 shares of a large oil company, and one oil tanker ran aground, spilling millions of gallons of oil, and the company had to pay billions of dollars for the clean-up and fines. Does this sound familiar? It should, because this exact thing actually happened a few years ago.

Let's suppose, on the other hand, that you still owned 1,000 shares of stock, but you only owned 100 shares of the oil company and 100 shares of 9 other companies. When the tanker spilled its oil, the oil company's stock would have dropped, but at least you would have owned other stocks to help reduce your losses. And chances are, if you followed our guidelines and bought quality stocks, the other 9 companies you own stock in aren't going to suffer huge setbacks at the same time as the oil spill. When you diversify, you protect yourself against unexpected disaster.

In general, the wider the variety of stocks and asset classes you invest in, the safer your investments should be. Unfortunately, it's a lot easier to know you should own stock in many companies than it is to be able to afford to do it. You can still protect yourself to some extent—although not as much as through actual diversification—by buying stock in companies like Grand Metropolitan, which are also known as holding companies.

> A **HOLDING COMPANY** is a company that owns a number of other companies.

By owning the diverse companies that we mentioned (Burger King, Pillsbury, Jolly Green Giant, Häagen-Dazs, Pearl Vision Centers, Alpo, and many major liquor labels), Grand Metropolitan has diversified itself and helped to ensure that even if one or two of its component companies goes bad, the others will be able to keep the whole relatively strong. Again, you can refer to *Who Owns Who in America* for information on holding companies and then check out the ones you might like in either *Value Line* or *Standard & Poor's*.

To sum up these important basics of stock investing:

1. Buy quality stocks.
2. Diversify your holdings.
3. Think long term.

Before buying more of any stock you already own, you should always ask yourself, "Is there another quality stock out there that will help me spread my risk by diversifying?" If you're honest with yourself and do a little looking, you'll almost always answer that question with a "yes," and you'll be better off for it.

MANAGING YOUR STOCKS

If life were perfect, you'd buy stocks as a long-term investment, forget about them until you need the money, and then cash in for a big profit. You don't need me to tell you that life's anything but perfect. As you will recall, even the best of companies can suffer serious setbacks which hurt the long-term prospects of their stock. There are plenty of good, long-term stocks that you could have bought, kept for twenty years, and sold for a nice profit because they remained stable, quality buys. But even with quality stocks, you need to pay attention to what they're doing in the marketplace.

You should also pay attention to the market as a whole so that you're aware of, and can take advantage of, any major changes or investment opportunities. It never hurts to check out good buying or selling opportunities. Remember, for instance, buying stocks on sale. You need to know when they are marked down to do this. You should be able to rely on your financial advisor to keep you informed about these kinds of developments.

If you aren't using a financial advisor, it's up to you to stay informed about changing market conditions. Watch the business news; read the financial section of your newspaper; become familiar with the business resources on the Internet, and/or subscribe to financial publications.

Earlier, you learned about buying quality and holding it for the long haul. You don't need to buy and sell stocks every time there's a minor change in the market. However, in the event of a market pull-back, you may want to consider adding to current stock positions or starting new ones.

The Economy and the Stock Market

Stock prices go up and down for any number of reasons from increases in the interest rate to natural disasters to trade wars. Stock brokers and traders have to be good guessers to be successful. Anyone can react to news after the fact. What the stock market tries to do is anticipate what will happen next from the information on hand. They're not always successful at this, and that's why there's always such a hullabaloo in the stock market whenever there's a major economic announcement or forecast.

For the long-term investor, these economic cycles aren't as important as Wall Street likes to think they are. If you're investing over 10, 20, or even 30 years, you're going to run across some down times and even some recessions. That's a fact of economics. And every time your stocks pull back, your first instinct will be to drop those stocks. However, even accounting for recessions and down-turns, the stocks in the *S&P 500* have averaged better than a 14.5% return over the past 20 years. To invest successfully over the long haul, you need to learn to look past these short-term down swings and keep your long-term goals in mind.

When to Sell

Of course, it's inevitable that there will be a time when you'll have to sell some of your stocks. Sooner or later, you're bound to acquire some loser that will drag your portfolio down until you sell it. There are no hard and fast rules here. Knowing when to sell a stock is one of the hardest things to master in investing, but if most of your company's product or service line is going bad and you don't like what they're doing (or not doing) about it, it may be time to abandon ship. Also, if other companies in the same business as your company are doing well while your stock is suffering, that's another good indication that you should start looking into a new stock.

Don't be afraid to cut your losses and get out if something like that happens to one of your stocks. If your stock drops from $20 a share to $15, it's easy to convince yourself that it's going to rebound. But if either of the above conditions fit your stock, you'll probably see $10 a share long before you see anything close to $20 again.

There's a difference between selling because of what is happening to a particular company and what is happening generally in the economy, for instance, if there's a recession. The prospect of a recession should not be a reason to sell. After all, no one can reliably predict coming recessions. Also, if a recession is the only thing holding your stocks back, they should be in good shape to rebound in price when the economy inevitably rights itself and recovers.

Sell Discipline

It's easy to get burned hoping that a losing stock will rebound. It's also easy to get burned hoping that a winning stock will keep on gaining before it corrects itself. I'm not referring to the normal growth of quality stocks over the long haul. I'm talking about a stock that shoots up suddenly, say, from $15 a share to $22 a share in a week, because of takeover rumors. Right there, you would have made $7 a share, and that's almost 50% growth. And if it keeps up, who knows where it might top out? $25? $30? Or it might fall back to $16 tomorrow.

If you're someone who likes to keep active in your stock portfolio, knowing when to sell is the key to reaping the most profits. It's also a hard decision. That's why many investors adopt what is known as a sell discipline, or boundaries for buying and selling.

You may, for example, choose 20% as your trigger. That means if your stock suddenly goes up or down 20%, your broker will automatically sell it. If you want to hold on for the long term, though, none of this may apply to you.

> **SELL DISCIPLINE** involves setting percentage gain or loss parameters at which you decide sell your stock.

How to Read the Stock Page

In order to keep up any of the stock management you've now learned, you need to keep track of your stocks and the stock market. The best way to do this is to periodically check your stock in your newspaper's stock page. Most daily newspapers have a stock page in their business or finance section, and they're all laid out pretty much the same. Before you can look up a stock, you need to know what exchange to look under. You can get these from rating services such as *Value Line,* as well as from your broker or advisor. Disney, for example, trades on the New York Stock Exchange, abbreviated NYSE. This is the listing for Disney from *The Wall Street Journal* of December 12, 1995. It shows information from trading on the 11th.

| 52 Week | | | | | | | Vol | | | | |
Hi	Low	Stock	Sym	Div	%	PE	100s	Hi	Low	Close	Change
$64^{1/4}$	42	Disney	DIS	.36	.6	24	12575	$62^{3/8}$	$61^{1/8}$	$61^{5/8}$	$+^{5/8}$

- Symbol (Sym)

  You'll notice that Disney is listed as "Disney" in *The Wall Street Journal.* This is how you would typically find Disney listed in most newspapers. Every stock also has a designated abbreviation, called its symbol, which you can find in *Value Line* and *Standard & Poor's.* If you see a stock ticker, you'll see stocks listed by their symbol. *The Wall Street Journal* lists a stock's symbol after its abbreviation.

- Div, Yield %, and PE

  These figures give you an idea of how the stock is doing. "Div" is the latest dividend that the stock paid to it's shareholders. Yield % (Yld %) is the dividends or other distributions paid by a company on its securities, expressed as a percentage of price. Price/Earnings ratio (PE), as mentioned earlier in the chapter, is determined by dividing a stock's closing market price by the per share earnings of the stock for the most recent four quarters. [1] These figures, like all the price figures in a stock listing, are per share.

- Activity

  The "Vol 100s," meaning "Sales in 100's" figure shows how active a stock was during the day's trading. The 12575 for Disney means that 1,257,500 shares of Disney stock were bought and sold on December 11th. You can see that they do quite a lot of business at the New York Stock Exchange.

- Price Change

  These are the numbers that we're most interested in when we pick up a stock page. We want to know how well our stock is doing. The "Hi" and the "Low" tell the highest and lowest prices a stock sold for that day. They're nice to know so you can see the price range the stock traded for that day, but the important figures are the "Close" and the "Change." The "Close" tells you the price of a stock at the end of trading, and the "Change" tells you how much today's close is different from

---

[1] *The Wall Street Journal*

yesterday's, if at all. Disney's close of 61$^{5/8}$ for the 11th is up $^{5/8}$ from the previous day. That translates into $.625, which is a decent one-day gain and no doubt made everyone who owned Disney stock happy. The 52 Week Hi and Low are simply the high and low watermarks for Disney stock during the previous year.

You'll come across other figures in newspaper stock pages, from yearly and weekly highs to earnings ratios. You'll also come across running stock tickers on CNN and other news channels. As a long-term investor, though, you don't want to place too much importance on tracking these figures every day. If you're worrying about earnings ratios or checking your stock every five minutes, then you're either beyond the scope of what we're talking about here, or you're too uptight about your stock, and you'll never make it through the 10, 20, or more years you should plan on keeping your investments. Keep track of your stocks, but keep them in perspective, too.

Market Indices

In addition to following your own stocks, you should also keep tabs on how the market is doing as a whole. Fortunately, the stock market has generated a few indices to help you understand not only how individual stocks are doing but also how the market as a whole is doing.

> The *Dow Jones Industrial Average* is the price-weighted average of 30 actively traded blue chip stocks.

The *Dow Jones Industrial Average* is the oldest and probably the best-known index of stock performance. You can find the daily *Dow* figures in just about every newscast and newspaper in the country. These 30 corporations' stocks are listed on the New York Stock Exchange. The *Dow* is a reasonably good indicator of how the economy and the market are doing. If the strong companies are doing well, it seems to reason that they will bring others along with them. *Dow Jones* makes sure to keep its list of companies up to date to truly reflect the most prominent industrial sectors of the U.S. economy. As a historical note, the *Dow* once consisted largely of railroad stocks.

THE DOW JONES 30 INDUSTRIALS

AT&T	*DuPont*	*Minnesota Mn. Mfg.*
Allied Signal	*Eastman Kodak*	*JP Morgan*
Alcoa	*Exxon*	*Phillip Morris*
American Express	*General Electric*	*Procter & Gamble*
Bethlehem Steel	*General Motors*	*Sears*

THE DOW JONES 30 INDUSTRIALS—CONTINUED

Boeing	*Goodyear*	*Texaco*
Caterpillar	*IBM*	*Union Carbide*
Chevron	*International Paper*	*United Technology*
Coca-Cola	*McDonalds*	*Westinghouse*
Disney	*Merck*	*Woolworth*

The **Standard &
Poor's 500** (*S&P
500*) measures
the aggregate
value of 500
widely held
common stocks.
It consists of 400
industrial, 40
financial, and 60
transportation
and utility stocks.

Since the *Dow* only includes stock from 30 companies, the picture it provides us is incomplete. By taking into account 500 major stocks from the New York Stock Exchange, the American Stock Exchange, and the "over the counter" market, the *S&P 500* gives us a much broader picture of how the whole stock market is performing. In fact, the *S&P 500* represents about 80% of the market value of all the stocks traded on the NYSE. One thing to remember here is, when either the *Dow* or the *S&P 500* goes up, that doesn't mean that every stock in the index went up. It simply means that taken as a whole, the total value of all the stocks went up. In practice, a large number of stocks move up and down, and a gain generally means that more stocks were up than down. One more important thing to note about the *S&P 500*: it's the index against which most mutual funds gauge their performance.

In a nutshell, indices like the *Dow* and the *S&P 500,* and other indices you might run across like the *NASDAQ-OTC Price Index,* the *Value Line Composite Index,* and the *Wilshire 5000 Equity Index,* tell you how various segments of the market are performing. This lets you compare how your investment is doing in relation to the appropriate index. In general, you want your investments to perform at least as well that index. When the index is down, your investments will probably be down too, but that's to be expected. When the index is up, though, you want to see your stocks right there, too.

Holding on for the Long Term

Investing for the long term is such an important concept that it's worth walking you through more specific examples. Long-term goals can't be met with short-term investments. Long-term investments *will* experience ups and downs, but they will also generally provide strong returns if held for the long haul.

Look at another example from Disney to help illustrate this. Starting in the 1950's, Walt Disney used to give his housekeeper a few shares of stock every Christmas, birthday, and the like, all the time telling her she should hold on to it for her future. Well, she took Walt seriously and never sold a share. When she died in the summer of 1994, her dribs and drabs of stock had grown into a $9 million dollar portfolio!

Everyone can't get in on a Disney on the ground floor, but you can buy stock in a solid company and hold it until you see a substantial return. If, for example, you bought Disney stock in 1974 and held onto it, you could do a testimonial for the wonders of long-term investing. A modest $1,000 investment in Disney Stocks made on January 1, 1974 would be worth $17,895 as of October 31, 1994. A little bigger investment of $10,000 would now be worth $178,949! That works out to a 14.85% average annual return, which is even better than the *S&P 500* over that period.

DISNEY STOCK INVESTMENT

	$1,000 Investment	*$10,000 Investment*	*Annual Growth*
12/31/74	463	4,633	-53.67
12/31/75	1,116	11,163	140.95
12/31/76	1,020	10,198	-8.64
12/31/77	943	9,432	-7.51
12/31/78	955	9,553	1.28
12/31/79	1,083	10,827	13.34
12/31/80	1,257	12,571	16.11
12/31/81	1,307	13,065	3.93
12/31/82	1,615	16,148	23.60
12/31/83	1,370	13,696	-15.37
12/31/84	1,591	15,906	16.14
12/31/85	3,038	30,384	90.80
12/31/86	4,678	46,782	53.97
12/31/87	6,449	64,494	37.86
12/31/88	7,201	72,014	11.66
12/31/89	12,326	123,263	71.17
12/31/90	11,230	112,299	-8.89
12/31/91	12,740	127,395	13.44

continues

DISNEY STOCK INVESTMENT—CONTINUED

	$1,000 Investment	$10,000 Investment	Annual Growth
12/31/92	19,239	192,385	51.01
12/31/93	19,181	191,809	-0.30
10/31/94	17,895	178,949	-6.70
		Average Annual Growth = 14.85%	

(Data from the American Funds Group)

If you take a closer look at Disney's actual year-to-year performance, you'll see some huge up and down swings, but if you stuck through the bad times, and fought back the urge to sell when Disney was up, you would have made out very well over the course of the twenty years represented in this chart. The key to that success, as I'm sure you know, was holding on for the long term. If you had set up a sell discipline to kick in and dump your Disney stock when it dropped 20%, you would have sold in 1974, gotten out with your $800 or $8,000, depending on what you originally invested, and missed all the good times ahead.

If you really do your homework and pick out quality stocks, you shouldn't be afraid to sit on them for 10 or twenty years. Your stock will move up and down, but the general trend for quality stocks should bring you a healthy, long-term return despite any short-term setbacks.

Reinvesting

REINVESTING means using any dividends or interest income generated by an investment to purchase more of that investment instead of receiving cash.

Another investment strategy is illustrated by the Disney example. All the return figures from the Disney chart assume that all dividends were reinvested.

For stocks, reinvesting means using your dividends to buy more shares of stock. There's no rule saying you have to reinvest any of your dividends, and many people use dividends to augment their income. For your long-term growth investments, however, you should always reinvest as much of your dividend as you can. Don't go hungry for a month just to reinvest, but don't take that trip to Tahiti instead of buying more shares. You'll thank me and yourself in the long run.

In the Disney example, the $1,000 investment would have earned $785 in dividends over the 20 years. That's a tidy little sum in itself, but if you spent that money instead of reinvesting it, your $17,895 of stock would only be worth $14,719. By not reinvesting you would have lost $2,391 that your $785 in dividends would have helped generate. And if you're like me, you probably would have spent that $785 on something like a vacation—a lot of fun, but not a great long-term investment. The lesson here is, with your long-term investments, think long-term with the dividends as well as the price growth.

CLASS NOTES

Carol and Chip thought they were doing a reasonably good job of managing their money. Carol, 53, makes $36,000 a year as a teacher, while Chip, 52, runs the family business, bringing in about $90,000 per year. They've raised three children, who are now married and out of the house, and they're particularly proud of the fact that they paid all of their kids' college expenses in full, without taking out student loans. In view of all the funds they spent on college bills, the couple was satisfied with their savings—$75,000 in a money market, $75,000 in a growth & income mutual fund, and $120,000 in their combined retirement plans. They plan to leave the business to their kids, so they won't be selling that for retirement money.

After attending my class, however, Carol was sure they could do better. She went home and told Chip all about growth and income and stocks and mutual funds. He agreed they should look into getting better returns out of their investments, so Carol called and set up an appointment.

Unlike most of my prospective clients, Carol and Chip came in knowing what they wanted to do. Probably stemming from her teaching background, Carol believed in research. She read all she could before they came to see me.

"We want more growth out of our retirement investments," she said. "We're looking at about ten years, so we feel we can safely invest in growth as long as we avoid the really volatile investments."

"I think you're right," I said. "There are a number of options that might work for you."

"To be honest," Carol said, "We're pretty set on stocks. We'd like to move about $50,000 from our money market into stocks." From her research, Carol had come up with a list of potential

stock investments. Both Carol and Chip were comfortable with the notion of investing in stocks, but they wanted to make sure they bought stocks in well-established companies.

"We don't want to invest in any start-up companies," Chip said. "Can you help us go over our list and maybe suggest some other stocks we should consider?"

"Let's take a look at your list and evaluate it in light of the things we've been talking about. Maybe we can narrow it down to a thousand stocks!" I said with a laugh. "All kidding aside," I continued, "it sounds like you have a very good plan, and I think we can come up with some stocks that will perform as you're hoping."

5 Bonds

Although you may all be disciples of growth by now, you still need to take a longer look at the income side of investing before you set your sights on the stock market. Income investments should make up an important part of most investors' portfolios.

WHAT IS A BOND?

Bonds are a way for business and government to raise money. Remember that when you buy stock, you buy shares in a business, meaning you actually own part of the company. With bonds, on the other hand, you don't own part of the company or government. Instead, you are loaning money to the business or government that issued the bonds. For bonds, that sum is usually in $1,000 increments.

In return, the business or government that you bought the bond from agrees to pay you interest until the time comes to pay back the money you lent them—the principal. Essentially, when you buy a bond, you agree to act like a bank for the business or government who sold the bond to you, except you don't get to set the terms.

> A **BOND** is an instrument of debt that pays interest over time and returns your principal at maturity.

> The **FACE VALUE** of one bond is usually $1,000. Face value is also called **PAR VALUE**.

The **MATURITY DATE** is a pre-determined date that the business or government who sold you a bond sets for paying you back the principal amount of your bond.

When you buy a bond, the business or government will specify how much interest they will pay you, how often they will pay, and when they will pay you back. The interest rate is set for the life of the bond. The amount that a bond pays is a yearly figure paid semi-annually. It is determined by a combination of the prevailing interest rates at the time your bond is originally issued and the risk involved in holding that bond. The date that they set to pay back your principal is called the maturity date. When this date arrives, your bond is said to have "matured."

The maturity date for a debt instrument such as a bond can range anywhere from a few months to thirty years, depending upon the type of security. Remember that the maturity date determines how long your bond agreement will last.

A **NEGOTIABLE** investment is one you can easily sell or trade any time.

Unlike CDs, a bond maturity date of five years, for example, doesn't mean that you are locked into that bond for five years and can't get your money out without paying a specified penalty. Bonds are fully negotiable, meaning that you can sell them at any time.

If an emergency, or opportunity, pops up, you can sell your bond on the open market. You'll learn more about selling bonds before their maturity date later in this chapter.

Bonds, as a group, have not generated as much return over time as have growth investments, such as stocks. With bonds, though, you get a fixed interest payment that's generally higher than those offered by CDs or savings accounts. Bonds are also an important way to properly diversify your portfolio.

20-YEAR INVESTMENT RETURNS

	S&P 500	Bonds	Inflation
20-year average (1975-94)	13.46	10.15	5.53
Last 10-year avg. (1985-94)	14.51	10.41	3.68

(Data from the S&P 500 index, the Lehman Brothers Bond Index, The American Funds Group Research, Chase Investment Performance Digest, and Chase Global Data & Research)

Face Value vs. Market Value

Most investors buy bonds for the income stream and usually don't think about the bonds until they mature. There's nothing wrong with this approach, but you should be aware of your other options. When you hold a bond to maturity, you will, barring any unusual circumstances, receive the full face value of your bond, usually $1,000. When you decide, however, to sell your bond before the maturity date, the market determines how much you will get for your bond.

> **Market Value** for a bond is the price, determined by supply and demand, that you can get if you want to sell a bond in the market place before its maturity date.

The market value for a bond can be the face value of the bond, but it is usually greater or lower, depending on the current interest rate and other factors such as the stability of the company or municipality that issued the bond, the bond's maturity date, and any call provisions.

Interest rates determine much of the market value of bonds. When interest rates go up, the market value of your bonds goes down. Conversely, when interest rates go down, the market value of your bonds goes up.

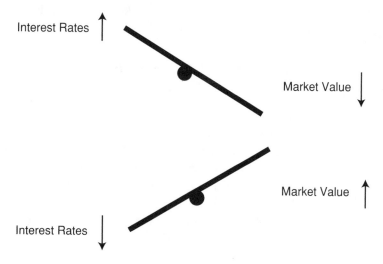

It's important to remember that this is for market value *only*. If you hold your bond to maturity, you will get full face value for your bond. Let's look at an example that will help explain this.

If you buy a $1,000 bond that pays 5% interest until the bond matures in 10 years, you will receive $50 each year for 10 years in interest payments, and you will get your

$1,000 in full when the bond matures. If that's your plan (and it can be a very good plan for most investors to buy and hold their bonds rather than trade them), then the market value of your bond won't matter. You'll receive your interest and your face value upon maturity. If you decide to sell early, however, then you need to look at the prevailing interest rate. Remember that the interest on your bond is 5%. If the general economy-wide interest rate when you want to sell is less than, say 4%, you'll probably be able to sell your bond for more than face value. That's because your bond that earns 5% generates more income than current bonds that earn only 4%. If, on the other hand, interest rates go up to, say 6%, then your bond would probably be worth less than $1,000 on the open market because current 6% bonds would earn more income than your 5% bond.

Usually, if your bond has a higher interest rate than the current interest rate, you may make money if you sell it. If your bond has a lower interest rate than the current interest rate, you may lose money if you sell it. If you decide to keep your bond to maturity, the interest rate doesn't matter and you get full face value.

BILLS, NOTES, AND BONDS

A U.S. TREASURY BILL is a short-term security, sold at a discount, with a maturity of one year or less, issued in denominations from $10,000 to $1 million.

When you see the word "bonds," the investment may actually be another investment option. In this book, the term "bond" refers to an interest-earning debt instrument issued by a business or municipal government. You should know, however, that the three classifications of interest-earning debt instruments issued by the Federal Government include: U.S. Treasury bills, notes, and bonds. Bills are larger short-term securities. Notes and bonds function in the same way—they earn interest until they mature, and you can sell them any time. The major distinction is how long they take to mature.

CALL PROVISIONS

Since interest rates move up and down over time, it may not always be in the best interest of a business or government to have certain bonds in circulation. For example, if you bought a bond from good old XYZ that paid 8% interest ten years ago, you'd be pretty happy with it if today's interest rate dropped to 5%. XYZ, on the other hand, wouldn't be quite as thrilled to be paying 8% interest on a debt they could finance today at 5%. If XYZ had its druthers, it would pay you off and then sell new bonds at 5%. Call provisions allow the businesses and governments that issue bonds to do just that.

Obviously, if you're earning 8% on your XYZ bonds, and XYZ calls them in when the interest rate is 5%, you're not going to be very happy. Even though you get all your money back, you're going to have a hard time finding another quality bond earning 8% if the interest rate is 5%. That's why you need to carefully examine the call provisions of any bonds you might consider buying. Not all bonds have call provisions, and not all bond issuers exercise the call provisions that they stipulate. The thing to remember is that they can, so you should always consider and understand the call provisions when buying bonds.

TYPES OF BONDS

Bonds basically come in three varieties:

1. Government
2. Municipal
3. Corporate

Again, all three types of bonds perform the same. This time the difference lies with who's issuing the bonds.

Government Treasury Bills, Notes, Bonds, and any other securities, like Savings Bonds, that you can buy from the government, are all backed by the "Full faith and credit of the United States Government." Government bonds also include bonds issued by federal agencies, such as the Federal Home Loan Bank and Sallie Mae funds, which are not directly backed by the U. S. Government. For all intents and purposes, any government bond is as secure as any other government bond, but those not directly backed by the government generally offer slightly higher interest rates to reflect the very small additional risk.

A **NOTE** is an intermediary security with a maturity of one to ten years, issued in denominations from $1,000 or more.

A **BOND** is a long-term debt instrument with a maturity of ten or more years, issued in denominations $1,000 or more.

A **CALL PROVISION** allows the business or government that issued a bond to pay you back your principal before the bond matures.

GOVERNMENT BONDS are securities issued by the Federal Government.

CORPORATE BONDS are issued by corporations.

MUNICIPAL BONDS are issued by states, counties, local municipalities, school districts, and other similar local authorities to fund local projects.

A DOUBLE TAX-EXEMPT investment is not subject to either federal or state taxes.

The government uses the money generated from bonds to assist everything from funding for federal programs to paying for the budget deficit. As you can imagine, the government issues quite a lot of bonds.

Many companies issue bonds to finance anything from corporate debt to new products. Both risk and return from corporate bonds can vary widely depending upon such factors as the strength and history of the company that issues them.

Local governments issue municipal bonds to fund projects like building new schools, roads, stadiums, or airports. Municipal bonds perform like any other bond, and they have the advantage that the interest they generate may be tax free!

Tax-Free Municipal Bonds

The tax-free status of certain bonds make them very attractive investments for anyone looking for a tax break. You never pay federal income tax on interest earned by municipal bonds. Municipal bonds are double tax-free when they fund projects in your state of residence, Puerto Rico, the U.S. Virgin Islands, or Guam. Tax-free, not tax-deferred! That means that if you live in Colorado and buy a Colorado municipal bond, you don't pay any federal or state taxes on the interest income the bond pays you. That's called double tax-exempt.

1995 COLORADO TAX-FREE INVESTMENT YIELD

Combined Federal & State Tax	Tax-Free Returns					
	4.5	5.0	5.5	6.0	6.5	7.0
	Equivalent Taxable Yields					
31.6% (28% Federal)	6.58	7.31	8.04	8.77	9.50	10.23
34.5% (31% Federal)	6.87	7.63	8.40	9.16	9.92	10.69
39.2% (36% Federal)	7.40	8.22	9.05	9.87	10.69	11.51
42.6% (39.6% Federal)	7.84	8.71	9.58	10.45	11.32	12.20

Franklin Tax-Free Yield Calculator

If you live in Illinois, though, and you happened to buy a Colorado municipal bond, you would have to pay your state taxes on the interest income, but no Federal taxes. As you'll recall from our discussion of rates of return, eliminating the tax burden makes any investment considerably more profitable. To get a better idea of just how important tax-free status can be, let's take a look in the above table at a few municipal bonds, their actual returns, and their effective returns after factoring in taxes.

That means if you are in the 31.6% tax bracket and buy a double tax-exempt bond paying 6%, your 6% tax-free return is equal to 9.16% taxable return. As you can see, the difference between the tax-free and the equivalent taxable yields is significant, especially at higher tax brackets. That makes municipal bonds very attractive investments when compared to taxable investments, particularly to investors with large taxable incomes.

One thing to remember about tax-free bonds: if you sell your bonds before maturity and make a profit, *your capital gain is taxable.* The tax-free status for municipal bonds applies *only* to the interest the bonds earn. Any capital gain you earn by selling your bond (if interest rates went down, for example, and you decided to sell because you could get more than $1,000 for your bond) is fully taxable. You never want to forget that when you consider selling a tax-free bond, or any bond, before its maturity date.

How Bonds Pay Interest

In addition to the three categories of bond issuers, bonds are also classified in two other ways.

Coupon Bonds

When you buy a coupon bond, the bond issuer is committing to pay you interest at regular intervals, specified by the bond. For example, a $1,000 XYZ coupon bond paying 8% pays $40 interest every six months, to total $80 a year. Furthermore, when your $1,000 XYZ coupon bond matures, XYZ will pay you the $1,000 face value of your bond. To help you remember coupon bonds, I've got a quick little story about how they got their name. It used to be that when you bought coupon bonds, they actually came with an attached sheet of pre-dated coupons. When the date of each coupon rolled around, you'd go to your local bank, get the bond from your safety deposit box, clip the current coupon, and present it to the teller for redemption. Today the process is largely automated, and coupon bonds are often referred to as registered bonds, but the principle stays the same. All you need to remember is coupon equals cash. *Coupon bonds earn you income on a regular basis.*

COUPON BONDS pay regular interest—usually every 6 months.

Zero-Coupon Bonds

ZERO-COUPON BONDS are purchased at a discount and accumulate interest so that, at maturity, they will be worth the face value of the bond.

While coupon bonds give you current income in the form of steady interest payments, zero-coupon bonds are designed to meet a *future* income need. Let's think about this for a moment. A coupon bond gives you *current* interest. A zero-coupon bond pays no current income, so it has no coupon (something that actually makes sense). At this point, I'm sure you're wondering where the interest goes if you don't get any interest payments. With zero-coupon bonds, the interest grows in the bond, which means that at maturity, the bond will be worth a lot more than what you originally paid for it.

That's in "financialese." More simply, as all of you shoppers know, when we buy something at a discount it costs less than the full price. Same with these bonds: when you buy them at a discount, you pay less than their "full" price (maturity value).

U.S. Treasury zero-coupon bonds are always worth a thousand dollars at maturity. But when you buy them, you pay considerably less (how much less depends on how many years that bond has left before its maturity date). If, for example, you bought two zero-coupon bonds, both with $1,000 face values and both paying the same interest rate, and you paid $275 for one bond and $750 for the other, which one will mature sooner? Right, the $750 bond, because it only needs to accumulate $250 more to reach $1,000, while the $275 bond needs to accumulate $725. We can figure this out because we have our rule about maturity value: all of these bonds are worth $1000 at maturity. For both bonds, all of the "interest" they earn will go toward making the bond worth $1000.

Let's turn our attention to that $275 bond now. In the fall of 1995, bond yields were running about 6.7%; $275 was about what you'd pay for a 20-year zero-coupon bond. That means you won't see one nickel of interest for 20 years, but in 2015 you'll be able to cash that bond in for your $1,000. The longer the maturity, the less the bond will cost you. But remember, the longer the maturity also means the greater the risk that interest rates may change and possibly lock you into a yield below that currently available in the market place. Should you care? Only if you will be selling the bond prior to maturity. If your goal is $1,000 in 20 years, the interest rate won't change the final return one cent.

Using Zero-Coupon Bonds

What all this means for you as an investor is that you can lock in $1000 for a future need without coming up with $1000 up front. Let's look at another example. Suppose you are going to retire in 20 years, and you want to have the peace of mind of knowing that when you leave your awful job, you'll have $25,000 waiting for you, come hell or high water. What can you do today to ensure that? You can buy 25 zero-coupon bonds that will be worth a thousand dollars each at maturity.

ZERO-COUPON BONDS

Goal: $25,000 in 2015

Buy: 25 $1,000 zero-coupon, 20-year bonds in 1995

Cost in 1995: 25 x market price = 25 x $275 = **$6,785**

Value in 2015: 25 x $1,000 = **$25,000**

If you buy 25 of those 20-year bonds, simply multiply the current price ($275) by 25, and you'll see it would cost $6785.00 in 1995 to buy 25 bonds which, at maturity, will be worth the $25,000 you want. As you can see, these bonds are great vehicles for planning for a specific future goal like college education for the children or your retirement.

In addition, as with coupon bonds, you can also sell your zero-coupon bonds before maturity without penalty. Again, as we saw with coupon bonds, the market value of a zero-coupon bond depends heavily on current interest rates. With zero-coupon bonds, market value will also depend on how long the bond has accumulated interest. If, for example, you wanted to sell that 20-year bond six months after you bought it and interest rates hadn't changed, your market value wouldn't be much greater than the $275 you paid for it. If, on the other hand, you wanted to sell it in 2014 with only a year to go before its maturity date, you would likely get close to face value ($1000), because it will have accumulated interest all those years.

HOW THE BOND MARKET WORKS

The bond market is very sensitive to interest rates. For bonds already in the marketplace, when interest rates go up, bond prices come down. When interest rates go down, bond prices go up. For new bonds, the current interest rate also helps determine their price. If a new bond offers a return equal to the interest rate, it will probably sell for around face value, usually $1,000. If a bond offers an interest rate higher than prevailing interest rates, it will usually sell for more than face value. This is called a *premium*. Conversely, a bond will usually sell for less than face value if its interest rate is lower than prevailing interest rates. This is known as a *discount*.

Bond Ratings

In addition to reacting to interest rates, bond prices are affected by the reliability of the bond. Like stocks, bonds are rated by independent firms. *Standard & Poor's* and *Moody's* are the two most recognized bond rating services.

BOND RATINGS

Standard & Poor's	Moody's	
AAA	Aaa	
AA	Aa	**Investment Grade**
A	A	High quality, reliable lower yields.
BBB	Baa	
BB	Ba	
B	B	**Junk Bonds**
CCC↓	Caa↓	Lower quality, high yield, unreliable.

JUNK BONDS are issued by corporations with no long-term record of sales and earnings or by corporations or municipalities with shaky credit.

In general, the higher the bond rating, the lower the risk, the lower the return; the lower the bond rating, the higher the risk, the higher the return. Federal government bonds are considered to be of the highest credit quality, as we like to assume that the U.S. Government will not collapse and will stand behind its debt.

This follows right along with what we've seen about risk and reward. The greater the risk, the greater the reward. It also explains how bond ratings affect bond prices. If you were offered a bond rated AAA, paying 5%, or a bond rated BBB, paying 5%, which would you pick? Not a tough call, is it? Reflecting this, the AAA bond gives you less interest than a BBB, so you have to make a choice based on risk and return.

Insured Bonds

Some bond issuers take out insurance on their bonds. These bonds are insured with private insurers for both interest and principal. That means you will get your face value back and all the interest promised to you, no matter what happens to the bond issuer. As you can imagine, this makes these bonds essentially foolproof—lower risk—and also drives down the yield they pay—lower return.

The important thing to understand about ratings is that bonds can be as volatile and risky as any pure growth stock out there. They can also, in the form of U.S. Treasury bonds, be the safest investment around. The market knows which is which and sets prices accordingly. You have to know what kind of bonds you want so you don't end up buying a junk bond for its high yield when you really want a treasury bond and its security.

Market Trends

Interest rates are very important to the bond market. When rates are up, bond prices go down, and vice versa. Interest rates, in turn, fluctuate with the economy. The Federal Open Market Committee (the Fed, for short) uses interest rates to help manage the economy. When the economy is slow, the Fed lowers interest rates to encourage spending and borrowing, which is supposed to stimulate business. When the economy is growing too rapidly, the Fed generally raises rates to slow the economy and keep inflation in check. Interest rates always affect bond prices the same way, so we have to keep track of them to understand the bond market.

BUYING AND SELLING BONDS

Most investors buy bonds from their investment advisor in a similar manner to buying stocks. Corporations and municipalities typically don't sell bonds to individual investors. Whenever a corporation or municipality wishes to issue a new bond, the major bond underwriters bid amongst themselves to determine the interest rate for the bond.

> An **UNDERWRITER** is an investment banking firm that, alone or with partners, agrees to purchase and distribute new bond issues.

Whichever underwriter bids the lowest cost to the issuer gets to sell all the bonds in that issue. Essentially, that underwriter buys all the bonds. In reality, every underwriter who bids on a large bond issue will already have several other investment banking firms lined up and committed to buy a large number of bonds. These firms, in turn, will sell the bonds to their clients—institutional and individual investors.

You can save money and buy Treasury bills directly from the Federal Reserve Bank, or the Bureau of Federal Debt at auctions, but the process is complicated and bureaucratic. Advisors will charge you a commission, but the process is far simpler for the investor. When you call your advisor to buy a bond, she will sell it to you from her firm's inventory if they have it. Major brokerage houses keep a large inventory of major bonds on hand to sell to their own clients as well as institutional investors. If they do not have enough of the particular bond that you want, they will go into the bond market and try to buy the bonds for you.

Bond Markets

There's no one place where bond traders meet to sell bonds. Some bonds are traded on exchanges like the New York Stock Exchange, but most bond trading is done over computers, along the lines of over the counter stock trading. Advisors use the same bidding process as in stock trading to find the best price for their clients. Again, the trading is highly regulated.

Investing in Bonds

Bonds are the classic income investment. If you want a steady stream of income now, coupon bonds are a good choice. If you don't need income now, but you want a guaranteed dollar amount for some point in the future, zero-coupon bonds are your best bet. Depending on credit quality and rating, bonds can offer you a relatively low-risk investment with a guaranteed return. You'll notice I didn't say "no-risk." As we saw with stocks, there are few risk-free investments. Remember, although we'd all like to earn lots of interest, the higher the return usually means the greater the risk.

Beating the Risk

As you learned with junk bonds, bonds can be every bit as risky as any other investment. If you buy bonds in a company that goes out of business or a municipality that defaults on its debt, then you could be in trouble. The key to successfully investing in bonds is to remember what you're after. The average investor shouldn't be out to make a killing in bonds. In coupon bonds you want reliable income, which leads me to my first, only, and most important rule when it comes to beating the bond risk:

If it seems too good to be true, it probably is.

If, for example, the current interest rate is 5%, and most bonds are offering around 5.5%, what should you think of a bond that promises 8.5%? Caution! There's only one reason a company or municipality would offer bond rates significantly higher than the prevailing interest rate: higher risk. As an additional rule of thumb, remember that the longer the maturity, the greater the risk. If interest rates go up, you may find yourself locked into a lower yielding bond. No matter what you might want to invest in, you've got to remember the risk: reward relationship—higher return: higher risk. That's not to say that some high risk bonds might not pay off. Just remember the risk side.

BUYING BONDS

Deciding which bonds to buy is at least as important a decision as deciding to add bonds to your investment portfolio. As I mentioned before, you almost always buy your bonds from an advisor. Your advisor is also a good source of information about bonds. To get your money's worth from the commission you're paying, you'll want to take advantage of all the information your advisor can provide you.

Getting Information

Moody's or *Standard & Poor's* are great sources of information about bonds. The trouble is, there are literally thousands and thousands of bonds floating around out there. If you just pick up one of the rating books and try to plow through, you'll never get anywhere, and not all bonds are rated. Your advisor, on the other hand, can help you narrow down the field to a manageable number of candidates from which you can choose the bonds that best fit your investment goals. Your advisor can also find bonds with specific maturity dates, ratings, interest rates, call provisions—any characteristics you want in a bond—and present you with a list of options.

If, for example, you asked your advisor for a list of AAA (*Standard & Poor's*)/Aaa (*Moody's*) rated Texas municipal bonds on February 28, 1995, one of the bonds on the list may have been from a school district in Texas:

State	Moody/S&P	Qty	Issue	Coupon	Yield to Maturity	Maturity	Price
TX	Aaa / AAA	350	ALDINE TX INDPT SCH DIST PSF	4.900	02/15/08	5.754	92.280
			Callable 02/15/03 @ 100.00		Yield to Call	6.143	

Many bonds on the list your advisor gives you will have the same format. Most of the headings are self-explanatory. "State" tells you where the bond issuer is located. This is important for tax considerations if the bond is a municipal bond, which it is in this case. "Moody/S&P" gives you the rating for the bond from each of the ratings services. "Qty" is the number of bonds that your advisor has available for sale. "Issue" tells you the name of the bond (who you'd be loaning your money to). Also located under the "Issue" column, you will find any call provisions listed. "Coupon" is the interest that the bond will pay you per year. And "Maturity" is the maturity date for the bond.

"Yield to Maturity" and "Yield to Call" are a little more complex. They represent the actual total return you would earn on this bond if you held it to either maturity or until it was called in by the issuer.

We'll delve a little deeper into yield when we look at how to evaluate bond returns.

CURRENT YIELD is the rate of interest divided by the market price.

"Price" is also a little deceptive at first glance. You might logically think that the price for this bond is $92.28. If you remember that the face value for all bonds is $1,000, this seems to be a great bargain. Unfortunately, the investment world doesn't always work logically, and with bond prices you have to move the decimal point one place to the right to get the actual price of any bond. In this case the real price for the Aldine School District bond is $922.80. Don't ask me why they do it this way; I couldn't tell you, but you'll want to remember it.

You'll also want to consider the price of this particular bond for another moment. At $922.80, it is selling at a discount (less than its face value of $1,000). Since its rating is AAA/Aaa, why would it be selling at a discount? Right, the prevailing interest rate must be higher than the interest rate that the bond is paying. That doesn't mean you automatically don't want to buy this bond. You have to consider the yield, but it is something you should consider when making your buying decisions.

Information about government bonds looks essentially the same as the school district bond, with the exception that you won't see a rating because all government bonds are considered to be AAA+/Aaa+.

Issue	Coupon	Maturity	Yield to Maturity	Price
STRIP	0.000	02/15/10	7.468	33.387

In this example, you see a zero-coupon treasury bond due to mature in 2010. This listing is again from February 28, 1995, and you should note that the yield for this bond is significantly higher than the school district bond listing because this bond's yield is federally taxable. You should also note that, because it is a zero-coupon bond, the price is deeply discounted ($333.87). None of these factors in and of themselves mean you should or shouldn't buy either bond, but they should help you evaluate the bonds in terms of your own investment goals and needs.

Evaluating Risk

As with stocks, check a bond's rating for the best and easiest assessment of a bond's risk. Both *Standard & Poor's* and *Moody's* employ a lot of full-time financial analysts and economists to track the performance of these bonds. I'm not saying you should just look to a bond's rating for an assessment of risk and stick your head in the sand. Researching the issuers of your bonds is not only a smart practice, but it's also a good way to keep interested in your investments. But unless you're hooked up 24 hours a day to the AP wire, the chances are pretty good that the rating services are going to learn any relevant information about a bond's risk before you or I will. After all, that's their business.

Take another look at the bond rating chart from earlier in the chapter. You'll want to stay away from anything lower than the BBB/Baa dividing line if you want good quality, long-term, investment type bonds. If you are extra sensitive to risk, AAA/Aaa insured bonds can put your mind at ease. Junk bonds, at the other end of the spectrum, can be highly speculative.

Evaluating Return

A bond's interest rate (or coupon rate) is not necessarily the same as the return a bond will generate for you. That is because the price you pay for a bond is not always the face value. This is where yield becomes important. Remember that all bonds have a face value of $1,000. The interest rate on a bond is based on the face value. For example, a bond paying 5% will pay you $50 annually (5% of $1,000). Even if you only paid $900 for that bond, it will still pay you a return based on its $1,000 face value—$50 dollars annually. Your yield, however, will be greater if you paid $900 instead of $1,000, because you're earning the same $50, but you only had to pay $900 for the bond.

We can calculate bond yield using the following equation:

Bond Yield = *amount of interest/purchase price*

For a $1,000 bond paying 5% interest:

$1000 purchase price

$yield = \frac{50}{1000} = 5\%$

$900 purchase price

$yield = \frac{50}{900} = 5.55\%$

Remember that both bonds have the same face value ($1,000) and interest rates (5%). The difference in purchase price makes for the difference in yield. Notice that with a smaller purchase price, the bond yield goes up. That's because you are paying less to earn the same amount of interest. You get more bang for your buck. Conversely, if the price goes up, yield goes down, because you have to pay more to earn the same interest.

Bond yield, and not bond interest rate, is the key to evaluating a bond's return. Yield gives you a far better picture of how your bond will perform for you.

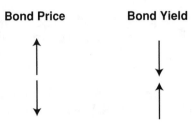

Bond Price   **Bond Yield**

Mechanics of Buying

As with stocks, when you decide to buy bonds, you generally have to buy more than one bond. This all depends on the bond you want and the firm you are buying your bonds from, but generally you buy coupon bonds in lots of 5 or 10. That means $5,000 or $10,000. For zero-coupons it's a little different. You need to check with your advisor for her firm's policy on minimum purchases. Don't let these figures discourage you, though. If you really want bonds but can't afford the large up-front cost, you can buy bond mutual funds, which we'll cover more in the next chapter.

Buying Quality

I can't emphasize this point enough: you get what you pay for. If you want a quality investment, buy a higher-rated bond. With bonds, the ratings services make the decisions a little easier for us. Through their examination of these bonds, the ratings services have determined that they are of investment quality, and their recommendations make good guidelines to follow. You can always go safer than BBB/Baa if you're risk-averse, but remember that as risk goes down, so does return. That's not a bad thing, just something you should always consider.

MANAGING YOUR BONDS

Most of us buy bonds for the long-term interest income. If that's why you want to buy bonds, then you don't need to be concerned about their day-to-day value. Some investors, however, buy bonds like they buy growth stock—hoping for price increases so they can sell on the open market at a profit.

How to Follow the Bond Market

Papers like *The Wall Street Journal* publish updates on some bonds, and you can try to follow your bonds there. Good luck. Unless you're a serious bond trader, it may not be worth your time and energy to try to decipher the system they use. If I want to know how a bond is doing, I punch it up on my computer and get a nice, easy-to-read summary or I call my bond desk. Since you generally have to buy your bonds through an advisor, you have access to this information, too. In fact, your advisor will at least send you quarterly account statements that update all your bonds. Let's take a look at one:

For the Period of 10/28/95 through 11/24/95

Municipal Bonds

Quantity	Description	Price	Market Value	Accrued Interest	Estimated Yield	Annual Income
25,000	ASPEN COLO	111.108	27,777.00	309.17	7.560%	2,100.00

8.400% 10/01/98

CPN PMT SEMI ANNUAL ON APR 01 AND OCT 01
MOODY RATING AAA S&P RATING AAA

These are the highlights from a statement for an investment in zero-coupon municipal bonds from Aspen, Colorado. The "Quantity" tells us we have $25,000-worth of these bonds at face value which, since we know every bond has a face value of $1,000, means we have 25 bonds. The "Description" tells us about the bond. It pays 8.4% interest semi-annually until October 1, 1998. This statement also give the bond's ratings.

> The **BENCHMARK BOND** is the 30-year Treasury bond.

"Price" is the current market price of one bond (this is listed in 10's which means that each bond is actually worth $1111.08), and the "Market Value" is the current market price for all 25 bonds that we own (25 x $1111.08 = $27,777.00; market value is *not* listed in 10's). "Accrued Interest" is the interest you've earned this year; "Yield" is based on the current market value, and "Annual Income" tells you how much you will make in interest this year.

If you're determined to follow the bond market on a daily basis, your best bet is the "Benchmark" bond. The Benchmark bond is the bond that you hear about on the national news every night right after the daily stock report. It is actually the yield of the most recently issued 30-year Treasury bond.

When to Sell

If you want to hold on to your bonds until they mature and don't ever want to think about selling, that's fine. That's why most of us buy bonds. You may consider selling your bonds, however, if the yield on your bond is significantly greater than the current yield of most bonds on the market. If you do choose to sell, you should be able to get a premium for your bonds (you should be able to sell them at a profit). One thing you need to remember, though, is that if you sell your bonds for a profit, you will earn taxable capital gains. If you bought your bonds for their tax-deferred status, you'll want to think long and hard before you sell any bonds to cash in on a short-term taxable profit.

Holding on for the Long Term

This brings us back to why we're investing in the first place. We want to meet our long-term goals. Bonds make excellent investments for many investors. They can provide current or future income and can help you plan for future financial needs. You can find bonds that match your own risk tolerance, and you can lock in a return and forget about your bonds until they mature or they are called. Bonds can make up an important part of your investment strategy. No matter what investment goals you want to pursue, bonds can still contribute to the diversity and stability of your investment portfolio.

CLASS NOTES

Clara is a 67-year-old widow. Her husband died 8 years ago, and they never had any children. Clara came to class because she's concerned about her living expenses. She received $100,000 from her husband's life insurance, which she put into CDs and was then able to live comfortably off the interest from them. When interest rates dropped, however, she quickly realized that her new CDs weren't going to make up the $570 difference between her Social Security check and her living expenses. Clara realized she'd better do something before she had to start drawing off of her $40,000 savings account and her $13,000 checking account.

Clara came into my office with an idea about what she wanted to do. "My friend Marge told me about bonds," she said. "She and her husband have some AT&T bonds, and she said they pay better interest than CDs."

"You're right, some bonds may pay you better interest rates than CDs."

"Well," she said, "It's getting so I can't make ends meet from the interest on my CDs. But are these bonds safe?"

"Bonds can be very reliable investments," I said. "You can even look up ratings for a lot of bonds to tell how secure they should be. Bonds from companies with strong credit ratings are generally very safe, and if you buy government bonds, they're as safe as you can get."

"So I should look at bonds from good companies and the government?"

"From what you're telling me," I said. "It sounds like you're a pretty conservative investor." Clara nodded. "In that case, I think these kind of bonds would make sense for you."

"Well, Marge's AT&T bonds seem a good place to start. I don't believe the phone company's going out of business."

"That is a good place to start," I said. "Then I can also show you some other bonds that might fit your needs, and we can start to make some comparisons."

6 Mutual Funds

WHAT IS A MUTUAL FUND?

It seems like you can't turn on the TV today without seeing some Wall Street wizard touting the latest and greatest mutual fund. Everywhere you turn, somebody wants to tell you about his or her mutual fund and why it's the best one for you to buy. Even your friends and co-workers can probably tell you why their mutual fund is the greatest thing since sliced bread. But how do you know if a mutual fund is right for you? How do you know if you want to include mutual funds in your invest-

> A **MUTUAL FUND** is a diversified investment portfolio that's professionally managed.

ment portfolio? As with stocks and bonds, you start with information. Let's start with the basics.

Essentially, the company that runs a mutual fund is like a huge investor. It sets invest-ment goals, parameters, and discipline, pooling the money from all the individual investors to buy the investments that make up the mutual fund's portfolio. These in-vestments can be anything from stocks and bonds to real estate or gold depending on the type of mutual fund.

DIVERSIFICATION

You should always try to keep your investments as diverse as possible. In fact, diversification is the greatest key to risk management. Unfortunately, you may not always have enough money to invest in enough individual stocks or investments to reach a proper level of diversification.

Mutual funds can help us solve this dilemma with what is known as "built-in" diversification. The average stock mutual fund owns stocks from many different companies—often well over 100 different stocks. That's diversification! With a mutual fund, each dollar that you invest buys you ownership in all the companies whose stock the mutual fund owns.

If, on the other hand, you wanted to invest in that many different companies on your own, you'd have to buy many shares of stock and spend a lot of money. As I'm sure you can see, that kind of investment is out of the league of most investors. Mutual funds give you diversification at a much more affordable cost.

PROFESSIONAL MANAGEMENT

Professional money management has long been available to the wealthy and to institutional investors, such as banks, large corporate pension plans, and so on. In the past, these professional money managers used to require accounts of a million dollars or more before they would be willing to handle a portfolio. Mutual funds make professional money management available to the average investor. Each mutual fund has a team of analysts and managers whose job it is to make sure that the funds perform as well as possible within the guidelines set forth in the prospectus. These managers make mutual funds very low maintenance investments because they assume the decision-making tasks regarding the portfolio.

Professional mutual fund managers also have an advantage over individual investors when it comes to getting information and reacting to it. They track down every bit of information they get a sniff of even before it hits the evening newscast. Again, it's how they make their living, so they take investment information very seriously. They also are in a position to be able to react to any breaking news almost instantly. They have the resources and the capital on hand to be able to buy or sell any investment before you might even hear that something looks good or bad.

All this about built-in diversity and professional management is not to say you can just buy any old mutual fund and then sit back and let the profits roll in. You need to pick mutual funds as carefully as you pick stocks, bonds, or any other investment. Ask yourself: "What kind of return am I looking for, and how much risk can I tolerate? Am I looking for growth, income, or a little of each?"

You also need to pay attention to your investment to make sure it performs as you expect it to. Diversification and professional management are excellent stepping stones to success, but they don't guarantee it.

INVESTING IN MUTUAL FUNDS

When you buy a mutual fund, you invest in all the investments that that mutual fund owns. That doesn't mean you actually own any shares of individual stocks or hold any actual bonds; instead you own shares in the mutual fund itself. Each share represents ownership in all the mutual fund's holdings. Your mutual fund shares increase or decrease in value based on the performance of all the investments that make up that mutual fund.

Net Asset Value (NAV)

Each share's value is figured daily, based on the market value of all the mutual fund's holdings at the close of business the previous day. This total value is divided by the number of shares outstanding to arrive at a per share value, called the Net Asset Value, or NAV. A share's NAV changes as the holdings in the mutual fund go up and down.

NET ASSET VALUE (NAV) is the market value of a mutual fund share.

The NAV is also the price of the share. You would pay NAV if you were to buy any mutual fund share (plus any sales charges, if applicable), and you would receive NAV if you were to sell your shares (less redemption charges, if applicable). Mutual fund listings in the newspaper show the NAV.

Mutual Fund Costs

While mutual funds now come with a variety of different pricing structures, three are most common. The first type is commonly called a "front-end" load. The load in a mutual fund is nothing more than the sales charge.

A LOAD is a mutual fund sales charge.

A "front-end load" fund will charge a sales fee when you initially buy the mutual fund. On your statement you will often see these referred to as "A" shares. For example, if you receive a statement, and it says you own Putnam OTC Emerging Growth Class A, that means you paid a sales charge upon purchasing the fund.

The second type of mutual fund is a "rear-load" or "back-end load" fund. With this type of fund you pay no initial sales charge; instead, the fund imposes a deferred sales charge if you sell your mutual fund before a specified period of time has passed. This type of fund is referred to as a "B" share.

So if your statement says you own Putnam OTC Emerging Growth Class B, you own this type of share. With this particular fund, you have to pay a sales charge if you sell your shares within 6 years of purchase (you can find the specific fee structures for your mutual fund in the prospectus which we will discuss later). As you can see from the chart below, this sales charge steadily decreases over the period of 6 years.

PUTNAM OTC EMERGING GROWTH, CLASS B

Years Since Purchase Payment Made	Contingent Deferred Sales Charge as a Percentage of Dollar Amount (Subject to Change)
0-1	5.0%
1-2	4.0%
2-3	3.0%
3-4	3.0%
4-5	2.0%
5-6	1.0%
6 and thereafter	NONE

A "no-load" fund, the third type of fund, doesn't have a sales charge, but that doesn't mean it's free. It wasn't until I started teaching my classes that I came to realize that people thought "no-load" funds were free. If they were free, that would make them charitable organizations, not professionally managed mutual funds. I find that many investors are aware of what a load or sales charge is with a mutual fund, but few are aware of other charges imposed by *all* mutual funds.

Do you think any mutual fund would manage your money on an on-going basis with absolutely no cost to you? Not likely. Mutual funds face expenses like the manager's salary, trading costs, toll-free numbers, statements, analysts' fees, and so on—not to mention the need to make a profit. Where do these dollars come from? They come from something called an annual expense ratio.

The annual expense ratio is expressed as a percent of the total assets of the mutual fund, and the mutual fund collects it every year to pay mutual fund expenses.

Some of you might say, "I've never been billed for my mutual fund." Instead, the mutual fund company simply takes this money from the fund's assets.

> A mutual fund's **ANNUAL EXPENSE RATIO** is the percentage of a mutual fund's assets used to cover the fund's expenses.

While there's nothing wrong with a fund charging an annual expense ratio, most people don't even realize that these fees exist. Furthermore, some funds also have what are called 12b-1 fees which allow them additionally to take a certain percentage of the fund's assets to cover sales and marketing costs.

Why do you think most people don't know about these fees? The one place they're spelled out is in a mutual fund prospectus. These are probably the most "user-unfriendly" documents in the history of civilization, but they contain all the important facts regarding any mutual fund you might consider. These are full disclosure documents and, as such, are very important. The sad fact is, though, very few people truly read them. In many of my classes, I ask my students how many of them own mutual funds, and the overwhelming majority of the hands go up. I then ask how many of them have read the prospectus for their fund, and rare is the class where more than one hand goes up.

MUTUAL FUND RISKS

Since mutual funds are made up of stocks, bonds, and other investments, they pose the same risks as the investments that make them up. If the stocks and bonds that make up your mutual fund go down, your mutual fund loses value, and your share price (NAV) goes down. While diversification and management help temper the risks in mutual funds, understand that they don't eliminate it. You can bet the ranch that no matter how well managed or diversified your fund may have been in a market decline like we had in 1987, your stock mutual fund would have declined in value. What is the key to managing risks associated with mutual funds? The single most important thing is to make certain that you are buying a mutual fund in line with your risk tolerance and goals.

Think back to the stock spectrum you read about in chapter 4. For example, just as an aggressive growth stock would tend to be more volatile than a growth & income stock, the same holds true for mutual funds. Aggressive growth mutual funds may be highly volatile. If you are the type of investor who would throw herself in front of a truck if your account value dropped, you are not likely to be a good candidate for an aggressive growth fund. Understand that the label describing your mutual fund—income, aggressive growth, tax-free—describes the underlying investments in that type of fund. If you understand which types of funds match up with your personal comfort zone and investment objectives, you'll find it much easier to pick out a mutual fund with a risk and return that is right for you.

A second way to minimize losses is to look at the quality of the mutual fund you are buying. Many people simply buy last year's "hot" fund. XYZ fund is getting a lot of publicity in the media, and your best friend tells you about her mutual fund (XYZ) that was up 40%, and you go to work and your boss tells you about XYZ fund which is up 40%. Soon you're thinking, "I gotta buy that XYZ fund so that I can be up 40%." Wrong! You can't judge a mutual fund by one year's performance. XYZ could be a great fund, or last year could have been an aberration. You have no way of knowing if you don't look deeper.

Instead of buying last year's hot fund, you want to buy a fund that has proven itself over the long haul. By simply buying a mutual fund with a sound rating and solid track record of good performance, you're lowering your risk. Again, any mutual fund can go down in bad times and up in good times. But if you look at a fund's long-term track record, you can see whether or not it performs well when the times are tough.

TIME HORIZON

As with so many of the other investments discussed in this book, it is very important that you purchase mutual funds as long-term investments. Remember the sin of stock investment—buying high and selling low. The same thing can be said for mutual fund investing. For instance, if you're buying a stock mutual fund, you know that over the years you'll encounter some volatility associated with the fund. If you're not prepared to see your investment through market cycles, you probably shouldn't be investing in this type of fund.

The structure of mutual funds makes them very well suited for long-term investing. Their diversification helps cushion the impact of sharp declines in individual stocks, and their professional management means they are continuously striving to maximize their performance. Finally, mutual funds allow you to automatically reinvest your dividends and capital gains as additional shares. This not only increases your principal, but when the market is down, you are buying more shares on sale.

TYPES OF MUTUAL FUNDS

Among the thousands of mutual funds out there, you can find growth, aggressive growth, growth & income, international, bond, tax-free—practically any type of mutual fund you could imagine. With so many different flavors, a table showing average mutual fund return would be meaningless. To get a meaningful picture of how a mutual fund should and will perform, you need to understand its investment goals and strategies. While not all of the types of mutual funds are included here, the most common that you're likely to come across and be interested in are included:

Growth Funds

Growth funds, like growth stocks, take a more aggressive approach designed to reap large returns over long time periods. Growth funds, in fact, are made up largely of growth stocks and perform similarly. They make good long-term investments, but they come with some risk. These funds focus on capital gains (another term for growth that you might see), not dividends (income). If you buy these, you should be prepared to hold on to them for a number of years to take advantage of their strategy.

AVERAGE ANNUAL RETURN, 1975-1994

Growth Funds	14.8% Average Annual Return
Aggressive Growth Funds	16.2% Average Annual Return

Source: Oppenheimer Funds

Income Funds

There are several types of income funds, including taxable, non-taxable, high quality with low risk, and high yield with high risk (junk bonds). These funds are designed to do just what the name implies: deliver a steady stream of income. Even if you don't need current income, these funds can be a good investment to help assure that your portfolio is properly diversified.

AVERAGE ANNUAL RETURN, 1975-1994

Income Funds	9% Average Annual Return

Source: Oppenheimer Funds

Balanced Funds

As the name suggests, a balanced fund takes a more middle-of-the-road approach to both risk and return. A balanced fund holds both stocks and bonds with an eye toward securing growth without sacrificing principal. A balanced fund generally won't pay as high a return as a growth fund in a good year, but it generally won't suffer as much of a loss in bad year. These funds produce both capital gains and income.

AVERAGE ANNUAL RETURN, 1975-1994

Balanced Funds	12.2% Average Annual Return

Source: Oppenheimer Funds

Specialty

If you have an interest in a special type of mutual fund, chances are someone has one out there to sell to you. These are sometimes called sector funds. You can buy mutual funds that hold only pharmaceutical stocks or only utility stocks. You can buy mutual funds that hold only U.S. Treasury bonds. You can buy tax-free mutual funds (these are funds that hold only tax-free municipal bonds). These sector funds typically concentrate their portfolios in certain industries and thus may have more risk than a more diversified fund.

Global & International

Any kind of mutual fund—growth, income, balanced, or specialty—can be a global or international fund, depending on what kinds of investments it holds. Global funds buy investments from all over the world, including the U.S. International funds buy investments only from countries other than the U.S. The benefits of these funds lie in their increased diversity and their ability to allow you to participate in investment opportunities in foreign markets. Over the long term, international stocks, as measured on the commonly-used Europe, Australia, Far East Index, have yielded good returns. Remember too our good friend, diversification. By spreading your investments among a number of different countries, you are lowering your risk again. You should note, though, that there may be other risks involved with these funds (currency and political, for example), so as always, be sure you are buying funds in line with your risk tolerance and goals.

AVERAGE ANNUAL RETURN, 1975-1994

International Growth Funds	14% Average Annual Return

Source: Oppenheimer Funds

Money Markets

You probably don't think of money markets as mutual funds, but a money market is a type of mutual fund that earns interest by trading short-term debt instruments like

T-bills and negotiable CD's. To the average investor, this means it works essentially as a savings account with a higher interest rate. A money market is an interest-earning investment with a constant dollar value. The value of your investment doesn't change—that's the constant dollar value—and you earn interest. Unlike a savings account, though, you buy shares in a money market. Each share is always worth one dollar, and your account is *not* insured against loss. This doesn't mean you should rush out and pull all of your money out of money markets. They are among the safest investments you can find. It's just something you should be aware of. You should also be aware that, since money markets are relatively safe and reliable, they may not pay you very much interest either (remember risk and reward).

BUYING MUTUAL FUNDS

With so many mutual funds out there and so many companies trying to sell you mutual funds, its hard to figure out which one is right for you and your investment goals. First, you need to figure out what kind of mutual fund you are looking for. That's the easy part. Then you need to sort through the vast sea of information available to you to find the right fit.

Getting Information

If anything, there's too much information out there about mutual funds. Every financial magazine offers their insights and tips. Every mutual fund company puts out literature and often commercials, extolling the virtue of their funds. You can even buy mutual fund newsletters from so-called experts with their best bets. Your job is to push past this marketing blitz and get down to the nuts and bolts of what prospective mutual funds offer and how they've performed in the past.

As we discussed earlier, all funds issue a prospectus. The prospectus describes in detail the fund, its objectives, share information, and fees. This is called "full disclosure" and is mandated and enforced by the SEC. In trying to provide full disclosure, though, these documents also tend to get very long and tedious. Remember, however, that the prospectus is the one place where you can find out all the important information you need about the fund, so you should read it thoroughly.

Use Your Financial Advisor

Mutual fund shares are relatively simple to buy. If you feel comfortable investing on your own, you can buy some mutual funds directly from the mutual fund company. If you would like help in the selection process, you can turn to a financial advisor. If you do choose to go to an advisor, you may pay a sales commission.

Remember, your advisor is there to serve you. Tell your advisor what kind of mutual fund you're looking for—what kind of risk and return you're looking for—and let her give you a list of options. Many funds, in fact, only sell their shares through advisors. I'm not suggesting that you blindly follow what she advises. Go through the information with her, making sure you understand her recommendations and suggestions. When it comes down to it, it's your money, and you need to be able to make an informed decision.

The Sales Piece

Typically, when you call a mutual fund company or an advisor for information about a mutual fund, you will receive a prospectus and a sales piece. Guess which of these two looks more user-friendly. You got it—the sales piece. Sales pieces are designed to get you to buy shares in a particular mutual fund, and you have to read them with that in mind. While everything a company says in a sales piece has to be true, you can be sure that they're not going to highlight the negative aspects of their mutual fund's performance. You need to read the sales piece carefully for any mutual fund you're considering, but you should remember it's their marketing device, and not an independent assessment. Use the sales piece as a starting point, but make sure to follow up on any fund that piques your interest.

Morningstar Reports

Once you've digested what the mutual fund company has to say about its products, it's time to get the lowdown from the independent experts. *Morningstar Reports* is one of the best known resources for information on mutual funds. *Morningstar* covers several thousand funds, providing a full page of information that includes information about performance, risk analysis, historical profiles, portfolio holdings, and a wide range of statistical information. *Morningstar* also provides information about the annual expense ratio. Guides are available from *Morningstar* to help you make the best use of their material.

While *Morningstar* is perhaps the best known, there are a number of other sources of information about mutual funds. It would be a good idea for you to look at several before making any final decisions. Financial magazines such as *Kiplinger's*, *Smart Money*, and *Forbes* provide mutual fund data and analyses. *Value Line* and *Lipper* also publish reports on many mutual funds. You can find many of these, including *Morningstar*, at most local libraries. If you do your homework, you'll find it much easier to pick a fund that's right for you.

Mechanics of Buying

Generally, you buy a mutual fund by purchasing a certain dollar amount—not by purchasing a certain number of shares. You tell the mutual fund company or your financial advisor how much you want to buy, and they figure out how many shares you get using the NAV (plus any applicable charges).

BUYING MUTUAL FUNDS

Shares = Money Invested/NAV per share + any applicable sales charges

If you invested $1,000 in a no-load fund with an NAV of $50 per share, you would end up with 20 shares.

Shares = $1,000/$50 = 20

You can invest any amount of money, but most mutual funds require a minimum initial investment of $1,000.

Dollar Cost Averaging

Basically, if you use dollar cost averaging and you want to invest $1,200, you could invest $100 a month for 12 months rather than investing the whole $1,200 all at once. The idea here is to buy at different times to take advantage of any price decreases. If shares sell for $25 one month but drop to $20 the next month, you can buy one more share for your same $100 in the second month. Dollar cost averaging can cut both ways, though. If prices started at $20 and went up to $25, you'd end up with one less share in the second month. You'd also miss out on the growth those shares would have earned.

DOLLAR COST AVERAGING means investing a fixed dollar amount at fixed intervals over a period of time rather than in a lump sum.

DOLLAR COST AVERAGING WITH $100 INVESTMENTS

If Prices Fall

Month 1

Share Price = $25
Total Purchase = $100/$25 = 4 shares

continues

DOLLAR COST AVERAGING WITH $100 INVESTMENTS—CONTINUED

If Prices Fall

Month 2

Share Price = $20
Total Purchase = $100/$20 = 5 shares

If Prices Rise

Month 1

Share Price = $20
Total Purchase = $100/$20 = 5 shares

Month 2

Share Price = $25
Total Purchase = $100/$25 = 4 shares

If the market is in a down cycle, dollar cost averaging can help your investment dollars go further. If the market is going up, however, dollar cost averaging can cost you money. Who's got a crystal ball that accurate? You need to weigh the pros and cons carefully and discuss them with your financial advisor before making any decisions.

Reinvesting Earnings

Most investors buy mutual funds for long-term results and, thus, opt to have their earnings automatically reinvested. Reinvesting your earnings ensures that you will see maximum growth from your mutual fund investment. On the other hand, if you want steady income, and you buy a bond fund, you may want your money sent to you. The decision is up to you, and you do have the flexibility to change the option you select (reinvest or cash) as your financial needs change.

MANAGING YOUR MUTUAL FUNDS

As long-term investments, mutual funds don't require a great deal of management. That's one of the reasons to buy a mutual fund in the first place. Again, though, as with any other investment, you shouldn't ignore your mutual funds. A periodic check is a good idea if only to keep you in the habit of following what's going on with your money.

How to Follow Your Mutual Funds

If you want to know right now how your fund is doing, you can always turn to the financial page of most newspapers or Section C of *The Wall Street Journal*. There you can find the daily quote of your fund's share price listed under NAV. You can even check the latest figures on your fund's 5-year return every Friday. These listings are by fund family then by an abbreviation of the individual fund, similar to stock quotes. Here are the highlights for the Oppenheimer Main Street Income and Growth Fund (A shares) from the *Journal* for December 12, 1995 showing trading from the 11th.

Oppenheimer A

MSIncGr A   27.12 + 0.05 + 30.9

These numbers are, in order, the NAV in dollars from the close of trading the previous day, the change in the NAV at the end of that day in dollars, and the percentage change in NAV for the year to date. (Note: Some papers report mutual funds differently, so be sure to check their keys.) For the Main Street Fund, the NAV closed on the 11th at $27.12. That's up $.05 from the 10th and 30.9% for the year.

Your quarterly account statements also update you on current pricing and other general information. Here's how your statement might look for the Oppenheimer Main Street Income and Growth Fund for the period of July 29, 1995 through August 25, 1995.

Quantity	Description	Price	Market Value	Dividend Option	Capital Gain Option
1,006.6	Oppenheimer Mainstreet Inc. & Growth Class A	25.340	25,507.35	REINVEST	REINVEST

"Quantity" here is the number of shares. "Price" is NAV; "Market Value" is the total value of all shares, and the "Dividend" and "Capital Gain Options" indicate that this investor wants to reinvest any proceeds that the fund generates.

When to Sell

Even though mutual funds work best as long-term investments, there may come a time when you need to sell or exchange your fund. If your fund is consistently performing worse than other similar funds, it may be time for a change. Remember to look at *similar* funds when making this judgment. Comparing growth to income mutual funds makes even less sense than comparing apples to oranges.

You might also want to reposition your fund if a particular market segment is doing poorly. If you own a utility fund and feel that interest rates will skyrocket, you'd probably want to think about getting out of that fund because utilities are very sensitive to changes in the interest rate. Most mutual fund companies recognize these contingencies and allow you to switch freely between their mutual funds.

ASSET ALLOCATION

Some studies have indicated that proper asset allocation accounts for over 90% of the performance in a given portfolio. In its simplest form, asset allocation means not only having stocks, bonds, and cash but also being in a variety of asset classes within those kind of investments.

An example or two might help to clarify this. When you think about stock mutual funds, there are literally thousands of funds that fit within that category, and they are all buying different types of stocks as we saw when we looked at our stock spectrum. The theory of asset allocation says you should own as many of these different types of funds as possible to be properly diversified in your mutual fund portfolio.

That means you should have one kind of mutual fund that buys small capitalization stocks (capitalization being the assets behind a company), one that perhaps buys U.S. large capitalization stocks, and another that buys foreign large capitalization stocks. Understand that when most of these asset allocation models define small capitalization, they are not talking about small like we think about it. They are talking about companies with a market capitalization under 2 billion dollars. (Doesn't sound too small, does it?)

If we take asset allocation one step further, we see that mutual funds often have two distinct styles of investing: growth and value.

Growth

Managers of growth style funds pay premium prices to acquire stocks that they think will demonstrate above average growth. They are not concerned about the current price of the stock; therefore, these stocks may have high price/earnings ratios. The theory behind the thinking is that it's worth paying expensive prices for these stocks if you believe they will continue to perform exceptionally.

Value

Managers of value style funds feel they can garner better investment results by buying companies that may be of somewhat lower earnings quality but that are much lower priced than stocks that growth managers would buy. Value portfolios, therefore, are frequently characterized by having stocks with low price/earnings ratios.

Asset allocation theory holds that it's not only important to own mutual funds specializing in different size companies but also to own mutual funds practicing these two different styles of investing because, historically, they take turns in outperforming each other. This means that if you want a truly diversified portfolio seeking both high total return and reduced risk, you should own both fund styles.

Because of the importance of asset allocation and the growth and value information presented here, many people currently have managed mutual fund portfolios with their assets divided according to both asset class and investment style. A good way to understand these is to think of them as a group of mutual funds that are professionally managed, often from different mutual fund families.

These accounts are managed so that the percentage of assets that you have in any one category will change to meet market conditions or economic factors. At any given time, you may have more exposure to small stock funds or foreign stocks or whatever the fund manager deems most likely to maximize your investment return. Many of these accounts require a minimum of $25,000.00. But given what I've told you here, you can go a long way toward recognizing asset allocation strategies in other mutual funds, and you can keep these in mind as you add mutual funds to your portfolio.

HOLDING ON FOR THE LONG TERM

For most investors, though, mutual funds work best as long-term growth investments. If you find a solid growth or balanced fund and sock it away for any length of time, chances are you'll see a substantial return on your money without the headaches involved in trying to diversify and manage your own stock portfolio.

CLASS NOTES

Peggy, 31 and single, has known for some time that she needs to take a long look at her investments, but she's always found some reason to let it slip. Her salary as a pharmaceutical sales representative is $46,000 per year, and she's been pleased with the way her retirement account has grown to $46,000. She also has an IRA worth $15,000 in mutual fund holdings and $10,000 in a money market. Peggy knew she could leave these funds alone until she got around to designing a true investment strategy. She just got a $4,000 bonus from work, though, and she's decided that now's the time to get serious.

"I want to retire early," she said after she'd given me her background information and shown me her portfolio. "Fifty-five at the latest. And I'm willing to take some risks to get there. I liked what you said about aggressive growth mutual funds in class. I think I've got the stomach for it, and my time-line is right."

"I think aggressive growth funds would be perfect for you, too," I said. "I've got information about a number of good ones that could suit your needs. And we can also talk about moving your retirement assets into more aggressive funds if you'd feel comfortable with that."

"That's exactly the kind of thing I'm looking for," she said.

"But you also want to stay diversified," I said, "even with mutual funds."

"That's exactly why I came to you," Peggy said. "I can read prospectuses as well anybody, but I want you to help me make sure I'm picking the right combination of funds. I don't want to end up with some hodgepodge of funds that sound great but don't give me enough diversity."

"I know right where to start," I said.

7 Retirement Planning

THE NEED FOR RETIREMENT PLANNING

If you heed the advice and information of only one chapter in this book, it should be this one. Planning for your retirement is perhaps the most critical financial planning you'll ever need to do. You can't plan for all the unexpected situations when you'll need money, but needing money for retirement should never take you by surprise. Everyone is going to retire some day. That means there is no excuse for not planning for it. And, since people are now living longer, your money has to last longer than it ever had to in the past. In addition, the future of Social Security is uncertain, and many of you can't count on the traditional company pension plan anymore, either.

It's no surprise that the single biggest financial worry of most people is outliving retirement assets. When you realize that 85% of all women end up alone and that the median income of women over 65 is $7,300 including Social Security, you begin to see the validity of that concern. How many of you think you could live comfortably on that little income?

The fact is, in 1945, 42 workers supported each retiree on Social Security. By 1993 that figure had dropped to 3 workers for each retiree. Many projections say that if the pattern continues, Social Security could be bankrupt by 2030. If that's not enough bad news, the latest changes in Social Security moved the age for full retirement benefits to age 66 starting in 2005. You can bet all your worldly goods that the requirement age will keep on getting older with future changes in the Social Security laws.

Also, recent studies have shown that a woman who reaches 50 years old without having had any serious illnesses is likely to live to 90. Do you think your financial assets can see you through to that age? If all these statistics seem frightening, they should! You should be very alarmed.

Too many people come into my office at age 50 worrying because they don't have any retirement assets, and they're thinking it's time they get started. The sad fact is, it's way past time for them. You don't need a fortune to start your retirement plans, you just need to start. And the sooner you get started, the easier it is to build that retirement nest egg. Here's a look at some of the tools that can help you plan for your retirement.

Managing Retirement Assets

Retirement is one of the most critical investment goals you'll ever have. The good news is that retirement planning usually involves a long-term investment strategy. As all of you know by now, "long-term" should trigger an alarm in your head that says, "Think growth." Growth-oriented investments, such as stocks and mutual funds, work particularly well for retirement plan investing because, by definition, they perform best over the long term.

One caution as you evaluate your options for retirement investing: In virtually all of them, you can't get to your money before age 59 1/2 without triggering penalties and tax consequences. That makes retirement plans even more suited for growth-oriented investments because you will be more apt to see your retirement investments through a variety of ups and downs and less apt to buy high and sell low. With retirement investments, you can ride out any short-term dips in the market and reap the rewards of long-term investing, as you saw in the long-term performance chart of the *S&P 500*.

Think Growth

Many people think they shouldn't take much risk with their retirement account. This isn't necessarily true. Remember the two big enemies: taxes and inflation. While investments in a retirement account grow tax deferred, they are still subject to the impact of inflation. Even with an inflation rate of only 4%, your buying power is cut in half in less than twenty years.

As a rule of thumb, the younger you are (and the more time you have until retirement), the more growth-oriented your investments should be. As you near retirement, you may wish to shift to more conservative investments. Then when you're actually in retirement, you may wish to switch again to a more income-oriented strategy. Bottom line: Look at your risk tolerance and your time horizon, make sure your money is working as hard for you as you are to get your money, and remember that your money will have to last you a long time in retirement.

Hands Off

Don't ever think of your retirement plan money as money you can spend. Think of this money as locked away in a foreign country that you absolutely can't get to until you retire. Not only shouldn't you take money out of your retirement fund, neither should you fine-tune your investments with every swing of the market. These are long-term investments. Let them work for you.

You need to leave this money alone—not just because you need it for retirement, but also because if you take any of it out you are usually subject to a 10% early withdrawal penalty (prior to age 59 1/2), *and* the government will tax any money that you withdraw as ordinary income.

For example, if you withdrew $5,000 from a qualified retirement plan prior to age 59 1/2, you'd pay a 10% penalty right off, which equals $500. Let's further assume that you're in the 28% tax bracket, so there goes another $1400. That leaves you with approximately $3100 of your $5000 withdrawal. Put simply, taking money from these accounts is too darn expensive. You're almost always better off getting the money you need somewhere else.

WHY YOU SHOULD SIGN UP FOR YOUR COMPANY PLAN

Even the government has recognized that retirement planning is a good thing for us to do and has given retirement plans some unique tax advantages that include allowing us to invest with pre-tax dollars and allowing our investments to grow tax-deferred.

> **PRE-TAX INVESTING** means that your taxable income is lowered by the amount of your investment contribution.

Here's an example of pre-tax investing: If you made $30,000 a year and put $3,000 into your company's retirement plan, the IRS would figure your "tax bill" based on an income of $27,000.

TAX-DEFERRED is a term describing an investment which postpones payment of taxes until you withdraw the dollars, usually after retirement.

Tax-deferred means that you don't pay any taxes on tax-deferred growth through the years while it is growing. You don't get a "tax bill" until you begin to draw the money out. The advantage here is that you'll typically be in a lower tax bracket when you're retired, so you'll have to pay less tax on your investment growth. In addition, you control how much you take out of your plan and thereby control the amount of money on which you pay taxes.

QUALIFIED PLANS

Here is a look at some of the more common types of company retirement plans. The traditional company pension is becoming a dinosaur in today's corporate environment. This means the responsibility for planning for your retirement has shifted from your company to you. That's where employer-sponsored retirement plans come in. Most of these plans allow you to put those pre-tax dollars in any investment your plan participates in, such as stock mutual funds, and they may also allow you to transfer your money from one company plan to another if you change jobs. If your plan doesn't allow you to transfer, stay tuned—IRA Rollovers are another alternative.

What is a Qualified Plan?

A qualified plan is a retirement plan that is set up by an employer, adheres to certain IRS rules, and allows employees to build tax-deferred retirement assets. When you invest in a qualified plan, you can buy many of the same investments that you would buy for your regular investment account. You can't get the money out of a qualified plan until you're 59 1/2, but when you figure the benefits of pre-tax investing and tax deferred growth, qualified plans are generally a win-win opportunity for you.

A **401(K)** is an employer-sponsored retirement plan which allows employees to contribute a percentage of their income, pre-tax, which then grows tax-deferred.

401(k) and 403(b)

Most of you have probably heard of 401(k) or 403(b) plans.

These are the best known and fastest growing types of retirement plans. As a matter of fact, investments in 401(k) plans have grown by 73% since 1989. When you put your money in a 401(k) plan, you really don't put your money into the plan per se, but rather into the investments that your plan participates in. These usually are a group of mutual funds whose investment objectives will range from the conservative to the more aggressive. You'll typically find a growth fund, a growth &

income fund, an income fund, and a very conservative fund as the minimum number of choices within any given plan.

Many people make the mistake of putting their 401(k) contributions into money markets or other low-risk, low-return investments because they are afraid to lose their retirement money and really don't understand their other choices. A major reason for this is that companies simply don't explain their plan or the available choices within that plan to employees. In almost every class I've given, someone asks about their retirement plan, explaining that they really don't understand much about it at all. It's no wonder so many people either aren't involved or make inappropriate choices.

> A **403(B)** is much the same as a 401(k), but it's for non-profit organizations, and the investments are frequently provided by an insurance company.

For your part, you need to know that your employer has a responsibility to make sure you truly understand your investment alternatives and to provide you basic education so that you can make informed choices. If you're not clear about your plan, keep asking questions until you are—your future livelihood is too important to be uneducated about. If you end up investing over the long term in these low-risk, low-return investments we discussed, you can actually hurt yourself because of our old nemesis, inflation.

Many plans allow you to invest the lesser of $30,000 or 15% of your annual salary. Don't be discouraged if you can't put the maximum amount into your plan. If 15% sounds steep to you, remember that over the long term, small amounts of money become very substantial sums.

Matching Contributions

Matching contributions are another reason not to miss the boat on investing in your qualified plan.

> A **MATCHING CONTRIBUTION** is an employer contribution to your plan, which you then invest as you wish within the plan's choices.

Essentially, your employer is giving you money for participating in the retirement plan. Again, not every employer offers a matching contribution, and the matching figures vary widely, but if it's there, you've got to take advantage of it. It's free money that, amazingly, companies will give you for your future. But if you don't save, they don't help. Don't give up free money!

I tell all my clients, no matter what you do, invest in your plan to get the full matching contribution. For example, if your employer will match half of your contribution up to 5% of your salary, and you invest 5%, your employer will give you an extra 2 1/2%. If, though, you only invest 4%, your employer only gives you an extra 2%. That means, on a salary of $30,000, you miss out on $150 free dollars! And those are tax-free dollars to boot. Multiply that by twenty years, factor in lost investment return, and you'll really start to see the beauty of matching contributions.

MATCHING CONTRIBUTIONS OF ONE HALF OF EMPLOYEE CONTRIBUTION UP TO 5% OF SALARY

Based on $30,000 annual salary

Contribution	Matching Contribution
5% of $30,000 = $1,500	1/2 of $1,500 = $750
4% of $30,000 = $1,200	1/2 of $1,200 = $600

A **VESTING SCHEDULE** sets out how long you must participate in a plan before you get credit for matching contribution dollars.

Additionally, your employer may have a vesting schedule for the match. Five years is a common vesting schedule. It's very important for you to know how the vesting schedule of your plan works. Depending upon the provisions of the employer's plan, few companies will credit matching contributions immediately; some will vest a certain percentage annually, but there is almost always a time requirement, which acts as an incentive for employees to remain with the company. Once again, ask your employer questions.

FULLY VESTED means that you've met a predetermined time period (set out in the vesting schedule), and all the money your employer has contributed to your plan as a match is yours.

Employers use a vesting schedule both as an incentive to keep you around and as a safeguard so they don't have to pay you all the money if you do leave before the vesting period is up.

Flexibility

Qualified plans let you invest freely in any of the investments—usually mutual funds—they participate in. They also allow you to change which investments your money is in (both money you've already invested and money you will invest in the future), generally at no cost and on a quarterly basis. This means you aren't ever wedded to one particular fund, and you can move your money within the plan's funds if you don't like how a certain fund is performing.

Let me remind you, though, that you're in this for the longest of terms—until retirement. If you're ever going to be in a position where you can ride out the ebbs and flows, this is it. Don't let the flexibility of your plan drive you to distraction by making you feel you've got to keep outguessing the market. First off, you won't be able to do it. Second, you're defeating your whole purpose. Get a good growth investment, and leave it alone (unless it turns out to be one of the real clunkers as discussed back in mutual funds). That way you'll get the return without the headache.

Transferability

Unlike a company pension fund, the investments you make in a qualified plan are also fully transferable. If you change jobs, you can take your 401(k) dollars with you and, if allowed, put them in your new company's plan. If you choose, you can put your money in an IRA Rollover instead. Any employer match you may have received may or may not be yours to take with you, depending on your company's vesting schedule, again, usually 5 years. Any of your money you invest, though, is always yours from day one.

If you happen to leave a company that offers a qualified plan, for self-employment or a job in a company that doesn't offer a plan, you can transfer your investment into an IRA (Individual Retirement Account) Rollover without penalty within 60 days. In an IRA Rollover you may choose from a wide variety of investments (stock, bonds, mutual funds, etc.), and the account continues to grow on a tax-deferred basis.

Taking Full Advantage of Your Plan

Putting money in your qualified plan is possibly the best way to start investing for your retirement for the following reasons:

- You get tax breaks.
- You don't have to worry about what happens if you change jobs.
- You have incentive to leave the money alone and let it grow.
- You may even get matching contributions from your employer.

If you follow the same, sound approach presented here, taking advantage of your qualified plan should put you well on your way to a secure retirement.

Managing Your Plan Account

Generally speaking, you should leave your account alone. Let it work for you. If you've picked a sound investment, you shouldn't have to do anything but keep contributing. Read your statements—they'll be similar to the mutual fund statements, with an additional line to track your current and year-to-date contributions and any employer match.

Like any other investment, if the market's down, your retirement plan investment will probably be down, too. You may want to change your investment choices if your investment objectives have changed, but before you decide to change your strategy, always say to yourself, "Remember the long term."

SEP-IRA's

A **SEP-IRA** is a type of retirement plan which allows you to put up to 15% of your compensation or $22,500— whichever is less—into a self-directed retirement plan.

In companies with fewer than 100 employees, only 6% have 401(k) plans. Let's face it, there are a ton of small businesses out there that just don't offer retirement plans. Fortunately, if you work for one of these companies, you have an alternative retirement investment. A SEP-IRA (Simplified Employee Pension Plan) can meet a lot of different needs. If you work for a small business, are self-employed, or earn money on the side in addition to your full-time employment, you should know about a SEP-IRA.

This means that your company can set up this plan and allow everybody to put a fixed percentage of their income away for retirement, letting it grow tax-deferred just like it does in a 401(k) plan. SEP-IRAs also take advantage of other nice features of 401(k) plans, such as contributions in pre-tax dollars.

If you are self-employed, you can even set up your own SEP. For example, if you work full-time for a company that has a 401(k) and you contribute to that plan, and in the evening you teach classes at a local university, you can still set up a SEP and put away a percentage of the income from the money you made teaching. Another nice thing about these plans is that they don't have any of the complicated reporting requirements that the bigger plans like 401(k)'s have, so they aren't expensive to implement and manage.

Another handy feature of these plans is their flexibility. If you're self-employed and have a wonderfully successful year in '96, you may want to make the maximum contribution. But suppose the bottom falls out in 1997. Then, in '97 you may want to contribute only 1 or 2% to your plan or make no contribution at all. With a SEP you can do that. You are not locked into a certain annual percentage contribution.

SEPs do many of the same things 401(k) plans will do for you and often offer greater investment flexibility. In 401(k) plans, your choices are typically limited to the insurance company or mutual fund that your company has chosen for your investments.

A self-directed SEP, on the other hand, allows you to invest in any stocks, bonds, mutual funds, and so on that you choose. If you work for a small company or are self-employed, I urge you to take a look at these plans. They can be perfect for meeting retirement planning needs for individuals or companies not willing or able to sponsor larger, more expensive plans, and they really are a piece of cake to set up and administer.

IRA's

An IRA, Investment Retirement Account, is another option available for building a retirement nest egg either in conjunction with or independent of a qualified plan. When you invest in an IRA, you are not buying shares of an IRA; you are buying investments for an account you declare as an IRA account.

With an IRA, you can choose the investments yourself, and you can buy or sell your IRA investments whenever you like, as long as you don't take the money out. For example, if you buy XYZ stock at $40 and sell your shares when they hit $60, you don't have to pay any taxes, as long as you don't withdraw the proceeds. The IRS knows they'll get their share later.

As with qualified plans, you are limited in what you can contribute to an IRA. Currently you can contribute $2,000 annually and an additional $250 if your spouse doesn't work. Don't be overly concerned about the specifics here because it looks like some changes will be coming.

All or part of your contribution to an IRA may be tax deductible depending on your situation, and it will *all* grow tax-deferred. Any money your IRA makes you is tax-deferred until you withdraw it, but the tax benefits aren't as substantial as with your qualified plan because the dollars in your IRA aren't pre-tax, like the ones in your plan. Congress is looking into making several changes to IRAs, so make sure you watch for any significant changes to the IRA regulations.

The Role of IRAs in Your Retirement Plan

You should generally view IRAs as supplements to the investments in your retirement plan, not as substitutes. Many people do contribute to both because of the advantage of tax-deferred growth. You also should consider that there's never any matching contribution for an IRA.

If, on the other hand, your employer doesn't offer a retirement plan, then you can put pre-tax dollars into an IRA much like you can with a qualified plan. In addition, depending on your income, you may be able to deduct all or part of an IRA contribution even if you participate in a qualified plan. Again, these rules may be changing—politicians aren't happy unless they're changing things. In any case, you will take care of your IRA and make your own investment decisions yourself, or with the help of a financial advisor.

Tax Advantages

Whether you are investing pre-tax or after-tax dollars, every penny that your IRA earns is tax-deferred until you begin to withdraw the money. That's the advantage that makes IRAs great retirement investments.

Managing Your IRA

You should treat an IRA the same way you would treat a qualified plan—find something good, and then lock it up. You can follow your statements to see how you are doing, but again, remember the long term. Your IRA statements, incidentally, will look identical to the statements for other types of investments you choose to buy. The only exception is that the top line may name your custodian, whoever is acting as the trustee for your account. Then the next line will say, "IRA FBO Your Name." That simply means "IRA For Benefit Of You"—technical jargon for "your IRA."

ANNUITIES

If you're looking for another investment that grows tax-deferred and that you know you won't need for a long time, then you should consider annuities. Insurance companies offer annuities to meet this market niche. Unless you're buying annuity type investments in your company retirement plan, you always buy annuities with after-tax dollars.

Annuities grow tax-deferred until you cash them out, much like an IRA or 401(k). Also like an IRA, withdrawing funds from an annuity prior to age 59 1/2 is a no-no and hits you with a 10% early withdrawal tax penalty. You typically buy annuities in a lump sum of $5,000 or more (up to $1 million or even more), but you can also start an annuity with a small investment and add to it monthly, depending on the company.

Types of Annuities

There are two major types of annuities: fixed and variable.

A **FIXED ANNUITY** pays a guaranteed rate of return.

At first glance, it might seem that the fixed annuity is a great deal with little risk. In fact, if you buy a fixed annuity from a high quality insurance company, there isn't much risk. Nor is there much return, because the underlying investments are tied to fixed income. You should know, too, that a fixed annuity is guaranteed, but the guarantee is only as good as the insurance company issuing it.

There are many rating companies that examine the financial health of insurance companies. These include, *AM Best*, *Duff & Phelps*, and *Standard & Poor's*. You'd be smart to ask for rating information before you buy a fixed annuity. Fixed annuities tend to attract conservative investors who want to know exactly what their return will be. Remember that inflation can be the biggest enemy in any fixed investment, including an annuity.

A **VARIABLE ANNUITY** pays you a variable return based on the performance of your investments within the annuity.

As you've probably guessed by now, you will see greater returns from variable annuities because you generally have the choice of several mutual fund–like investments that hold stocks and bonds. In a variable annuity you can choose investment vehicles that range from very conservative, acting almost like fixed annuities, to very aggressive, growth-oriented funds.

To understand the distinction between the two types of annuities you just need to look at how they perform. A fixed annuity acts almost like a CD that grows tax-deferred and is issued by an insurance company. For example, Hartford Insurance Company may say they will guarantee you a return of 6% over the next 7 years. That would be a fixed annuity.

On the other hand, variable annuities offer professionally managed portfolios that typically invest in stocks and bonds, similar to mutual funds, whose value fluctuates with values in the market. Generally, a major mutual fund company, *not* the issuing insurance company, manages these funds.

There a couple of wrinkles in variable annuities that you should know about. Commonly, with a variable annuity you have what is called "death in a down market protection." Here's what that means: Let's say you put $10,000 in a very aggressive fund within a variable annuity. Two years after you buy it the market has a major pull-back, and your $10,000 is suddenly worth $8,000. To top it all off, you're hit by lightning and killed. Your estate, though saddened by your sudden demise, will typically receive the higher of current market value ($8,000), which is the original purchase price ($10,000) of your annuity less any applicable fees. In this example your heirs would have received $10,000 even though your account value may have been $8,000, and they would have thanked you mightily.

Many annuities are also adding a feature called a "stepped up death benefit" (more fun insurance lingo). Using the above example, assume your $10,000 annuity has now appreciated to $18,000. On the anniversary date of your contract, the insurance company "steps up" the death benefit your beneficiaries will receive to that $18,000 mark. Henceforth, if your contract value goes down, your estate is assured of receiving that new high water mark of $18,000. Some companies do this annually, some every five years, so you will want to get the specifics on any annuity you consider.

Annuity Costs

Insurance companies certainly are not giving you something for nothing with annuities. These bells and whistles that are features of annuities come at a cost. That cost is higher annual expenses as compared to mutual funds that aren't part of an annuity. You need to decide if there's value there for you.

> A SURRENDER FEE is a penalty you pay for taking your money out of an annuity before a pre-determined period of time expires.

The most common fees associated with an annuity are called surrender fees, or penalties for early withdrawal.

A typical charge maybe 7% in the first year, declining 1% each year until there is no longer a fee. This is *in addition* to the early withdrawal tax penalty which we've already discussed. This is why annuities are appropriate for money you are *certain* you will leave alone for a long period of time.

You should note that the annuities are deferred, meaning they don't pay you until you start withdrawing from them. There are other kinds of annuities called "immediate annuities" which begin paying immediately upon purchasing. These are generally used as income programs which provide an assured tax-favored income stream; a portion of each payment is tax-free because it is considered return of principal. The rate of return on immediate annuities is typically very low, so you should only consider them in special situations. Always get as much information as possible on any annuity you are considering so you understand its features and potential drawbacks and can make sure the fit is right for you.

Managing Your Annuity

If you buy annuities, buy quality, buy for the long haul, and periodically check their performance. But for the most part, leave them alone. You will typically receive quarterly statements from the insurance company holding your annuity. These statements will tell you your overall account value, if it's a variable annuity, and which funds you're in. They may also give you a toll-free number that you should feel free to use if you have any questions. You should be comfortable asking the person who sold you the annuity anything you want to know about performance, statements, and so forth.

Overall Approach

A successful retirement plan will probably make use of many of these types of vehicles, as well as other stock, bond, and mutual fund investments. The key is to always remind yourself that you're looking for long-term results and growth. Don't get scared by short-term setbacks. When you're investing for the long term, you can afford to ride out the market and take advantage of those growth returns we looked at earlier. Maximize all the tax-breaks you can find, and by all means, take advantage of any and all matching contributions your employer might offer. Most important, start investing now. Every day you wait is one less day that your money isn't working for you.

Cost of Not Investing

Let's look at two families, the Simmons and the Wilsons, who are all the same age. Both make $4,000 annual contributions to their 401(k) plans for 20 years and earn a 10% average annual return on their money. The Simmons start at age 36 and stop at age 55. The Wilsons, on the other hand, start at age 46 and contribute until age 65. By age 65 they've both contributed $80,000. The Simmons' 401(k) account is worth $653,649, but the Wilsons' account is only worth $252,010. That's $401,639 difference, and the Wilsons only waited 10 years!

401(k) Plans

	Simmons	Wilsons
Annual Contributions:	$4,000	$4,000
Age:	36–55	46–65
Average Annual Return:	10%	10%
Value of Account at age 65:	**$653,649**	**$252,010**

Age	Simmons' Cumulative Investment	Total Value at 10% Annual Return	Wilsons' Cumulative Investment	Total Value at 10% Annual Return
36	$4,000	$4,400		
37	8,000	9,240		
38	12,000	14,564		

continues

401(k) PLANS—CONTINUED

Age	Simmons' Cumulative Investment	Total Value at 10% Annual Return	Wilsons' Cumulative Investment	Total Value at 10% Annual Return
39	16,000	20,420		
40	20,000	26,862		
41	24,000	33,949		
42	28,000	41,744		
43	32,000	50,318		
44	36,000	59,750		
45	40,000	70,125		
46	44,000	81,537	4,000	$4,400
47	48,000	94,091	8,000	9,240
48	52,000	107,900	12,000	14,564
49	56,000	123,090	16,000	20,420
50	60,000	139,799	20,000	26,862
51	64,000	158,179	24,000	33,949
52	68,000	178,397	28,000	41,744
53	72,000	200,637	32,000	50,318
54	76,000	225,100	36,000	59,750
55	80,000	252,010	40,000	70,125
56		277,211	44,000	81,537
57		304,932	48,000	94,091
58		335,425	52,000	107,900
59		368,968	56,000	123,090
60		405,865	60,000	139,799
61		446,451	64,000	158,179
62		491,096	68,000	178,397
63		540,206	72,000	200,637
64		594,226	76,000	225,100
65		653,649	80,000	252,010
Ending Value	**$80,000**	**$653,649**	**$80,000**	**$252,010**

Data from the Aim Family of Funds, 1995

That's a pretty convincing picture about the cost of waiting to start your retirement planning, isn't it?

CLASS NOTES

Donna and her husband Dennis are both 46 years old. Donna makes $38,000 a year as a nurse, and Dennis makes $36,000 working for the city as a social worker. Amanda, their only daughter, is 24 and single. She just started a new job as a copy editor where she makes $21,000 per year. She has $1,000 from graduation presents in a savings account, and she is not yet eligible to participate in her retirement plan. Donna and Dennis have $15,000 in a savings account, and Dennis contributes 10% of his salary to the city's retirement plan. Donna does not participate in her retirement plan.

Donna came to the class because she and Dennis had begun to worry about their retirement. She brought Amanda with her.

Donna and Dennis had read about the problems with Social Security, and that prompted them to take a look at their own retirement assets. Unfortunately, they were in for a rude surprise because, based on their current savings and investments, it seemed unlikely that they would be able to retire before age 65, and even then they'd have to alter their lifestyle. They've always assumed that Dennis's retirement plan would provide enough to live on, and they've followed their parents' advice by investing money in their house rather than market investments. Now they're worried that they've waited too long.

"What can we do?" Donna asked me when the three of them came to see me.

I began to explain their options. "For one, Donna, you really ought to start contributing to your retirement plan."

"We thought about that," Donna said, "but I thought it was too late. I figured I'd be better off just building up our savings so we'd have something to live off of."

"You remember what I said about growth and savings versus taxes and inflation?" I asked.

"Yes," Amanda said, "over the long haul you need growth to avoid losing money to taxes and inflation."

"Right," I said, "and if you keep your money in savings, over the long term you won't get the growth you need to outperform inflation."

"But we're already 46," Donna said.

"And when do you want to retire?"

"We were hoping for around 60."

"That still gives you at least 15 years for growth," I pointed out. "That's plenty of time to make it worthwhile. Remember, this is money you're not going to touch until you retire, so you can ride out any temporary market drops."

"Yes," Donna said, "I remember the 10-year growth returns you told us about in class. When you think of it that way it does make sense."

"So then," Dennis added, "you'd probably recommend that we move our savings into growth investments, too. Right?"

"Well," I said, "leave enough in savings so that you feel comfortable. But remember, every dollar you put into a growth investment is a dollar that's working a lot harder for you."

"What about volatility?" Donna asked.

"The market moves in cycles. It's going to go down sometimes; but remember, you're in it for the long term."

"That does make sense," Dennis said. Donna agreed.

"That's all well and good," Amanda said, "but how does this apply to me? I'm not going retire for like 40 years."

"I'd recommend you start contributing to your retirement plan as soon as you're eligible," I said. "In the meantime, remember that chart I showed you in class with the long-term return from investing as little as $25 a month?"

"Yes," Amanda said, "that was pretty impressive."

"Well, you're young enough to start with a small investment from your savings, add small amounts to it like that, and just let it build. With your time frame, you could even look for more aggressive growth investments."

"I suppose I could afford $25 a month," Amanda said.

"Any investment is a good start," I said.

8 Speculative *Investments*

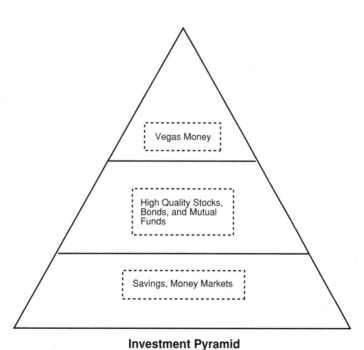

Investment Pyramid

You will often see investments grouped in something called an Investment Pyramid. An investment pyramid uses lower risk investments to form its foundation, much as they would form your financial foundation. These are investments like money markets, savings accounts, and so on. In the middle of the investment pyramid you'll find high quality stocks, mutual funds, and the like. You'll find the highest risk investments at the top of the pyramid.

View the highest risk investments as "Vegas" money. When you arrive at your local airport on your return trip from Las Vegas, it's highly likely that your money remained in Las Vegas. The theory is that you should only take as much money as you are prepared to lose.

SPECULATIVE INVESTMENTS offer potentially high returns but also inherently pose a higher than average risk of principal loss.

This also makes a good approach to speculative investments. There is nothing inherently wrong with speculative investments as long as you understand the high risk associated with them. However, you should be forewarned that despite what you may hear from financial advisors, friends, or relatives, these investments are never "sure winners." You'd better do your homework and make certain you're knowledgeable before leaping into this category.

The two phrases you want to note in this definition are high potential return and high risk. Investors buy speculative investments because of the lure of high returns or the promise of getting rich quick. Professionals can make a lot of money in speculation over the long term. But these professionals know how to limit their losses by using a number of sophisticated techniques and devices which the average investor doesn't even begin to understand.

Speculative investing is not for beginners. It's hard to find a lot of information about these investments, and much of the knowledge you need takes years to acquire. In fact, some of these investments are so complex and volatile that you have to be able to document your expertise *and* meet a required level of net worth before you even are allowed to trade in these instruments. Assuming you're now warned, here's a look at a few speculative investments you might run across.

COMMODITIES

When you speculate in commodities, you purchase something called a futures contract. When you buy or sell a futures contract, you hope that something will happen in the market that will make the product go up or down in price.

For example, if you bought orange juice futures in the hope that prices would go up, and a hard freeze in Florida and California killed off most of the oranges, you'd be very happy because there would be a lot less orange juice on the market. That would drive the price of orange juice up and build more gain into your contract. If on the other hand, a laboratory in Peoria, Illinois devised a method to make synthetic orange juice at a fraction of the cost of the real item, you would be unhappy.

This example is a little extreme, but it gives you an idea of the kinds of things that affect profit and loss in the futures market. By the way, farmers have been using the futures market for a long time to hedge their bets against crop loss, changes in the weather, and so on.

COMMODITIES are simple things like pork bellies, orange juice, oil, and wheat.

A FUTURES CONTRACT is an agreement to buy or sell a specific amount of a commodity or financial instrument at a particular price on a specified future date.

PENNY STOCKS

Let me start by confessing that I have a built-in bias against penny stocks. During the late 1970's, Denver was a big local market for over the counter penny stocks. There was huge speculative activity in penny stocks, particularly oil, gas, and gold-mining stocks. These stocks soared when they began trading on the market. There have been a number of lawsuits which have indicated that the qualities of the companies being touted didn't justify the rapid increase in price. Remember "Buyer Beware" when looking at this highly volatile, risky arena.

PENNY STOCKS are stocks that typically sell for less than one dollar per share.

In fact, I usually have at least one person who's been badly burned in the penny stock market in almost every class and seminar I give. Frequently these local markets follow a boom/bust cycle, and when I say "bust," I mean bust. Unfortunately, many inexperienced investors who got burned by these low quality stocks now understandably assume that all stock brokers and financial advisors are unscrupulous and that the stock market is an excellent way to throw your money away. Now that you've read this book, you know better, but many people lost so much that to this day it's hard for them to move forward with their investments.

Penny stocks themselves typically come from companies with a very limited or an unpredictable history of earnings and product development. Often, with penny stocks you are actually buying the management, banking on your belief in their ability to pull off their business concept and make money. There have been so many problems with the sale of these stocks to the public that there are many rules covering their presentation and sale. If you get a wonderful sales pitch about one of these from a "cold caller," you should think long and hard before investing any money based on verbal promises.

REAL ESTATE

Investing in real estate refers to properties other than your home that you might consider buying as an investment. When you buy real estate as an investment, you're hoping that the economics of the location will drive up the property values far more than they would otherwise rise. For example, if you bought land in Hawaii fifteen or twenty years ago, you're laughing all the way to your bank. If, however, you bought land in Texas during the oil boom, you're crying in your crude oil.

As many of you know, real estate is a high-ticket item that can be very volatile. If you're comfortable with that, real estate can be a great diversifying addition to your portfolio. Make sure, though, that you understand what and where you're buying, and talk to your accountant about possible tax consequences.

OPTIONS

Option strategies range from the conservative to the highly speculative, and not all options are created equal. Some option strategies are used very frequently by investors to enhance the return on their investment. Others involve highly sophisticated strategies used most often by investment professionals. When you buy an option, you are not really buying an investment. You are buying the right to buy or sell that investment in exchange for a certain price.

Here's an example to show you how option trading works: Let's say Heidi's Hot-dogs, Inc., is currently selling for $25 a share on the New York Stock Exchange. You feel that her stock will probably double over the next year. You can purchase an option on this stock at $35 a share in the next six months. This means you could buy the stock for $35 at any time during the next six months, even if the price of the stock went higher than $35. In exchange for this option, you would pay a certain premium, $2 per share ($200 for 100 shares).

You watch the stock start to go up, and you see the stock hit $45 a share within your 6-month time period. You then may exercise your option and buy that stock from the seller of the option for $35 a share even though the current market price is $45 a share.

On the other hand, if the stock doesn't hit your option price of $35 a share, then you don't have to buy that stock, but you do forfeit the money you paid to buy the option in the first place.

If you find this confusing, you're not alone. Options trading is one of the more complex market strategies. In fact, before you're allowed to trade options, you must meet certain requirements and sign an option agreement through the firm where you trade.

DERIVATIVES

Derivatives are really complicated investments that you, in all likelihood, will never invest in yourself. However, because of all the publicity derivatives have received lately, you should at least understand how they work.

> **DERIVATIVES** are specifically designed investments whose performance is tied to the performance of another security or investment.

A derivative, for example, may be some kind of investment that rises or falls in value based on the performance of an underlying index or by changes in the value of the U.S. dollar against one or more foreign currencies. These, like most of the other investments, can enhance the return or minimize the downside of investment portfolios if properly utilized by professional money managers, who, theoretically, have the research and sophistication in complex financial instruments to successfully deal in this arena (which the average investor doesn't have).

Although, problems in Orange County, California illustrate that even professionals are not immune to disaster when using these highly complex financial tools. The lack of understanding of these instruments and the risks involved essentially forced Orange County into bankruptcy.

ROLLING THE DICE

Now you have a very basic understanding of the most common speculative investments. But you really need more information before you start investing in any of these speculative investments. If, however, you have the time, aptitude, and inclination to become an expert in any of these arenas, these investments can pay off nicely. But they can still go sour on you, even if you know what you are doing. With speculative investments, just keep that "Vegas money" idea mind, and you'll do all right.

9 Investment *Advisors*

Whitney Boucher is a real broker with PaineWebber. *Smart Money* magazine followed him around for a week, and this is part of his story ("What Makes Whitney Run?" John Anderson, *Smart Money*, December 1995, pp. 106-115).

> *Whitney's driving force is his "gross production goal," the amount of fees he needs to earn for PaineWebber. His goal was $39,000 in gross production for the month of the interview. Since he earns roughly 1% commission on assets he manages, that means he needed to pull in about $3.9 million in assets. If he didn't consistently make his goal, he'd be "outta there" like the other "losers" who pass through PaineWebber on their way to another career. When Smart Money showed up, Whitney was worried, because he needed to bring in another $29,100 in gross production in the remaining 11 business days of the month, but he wasn't too worried. "At the end of the month, it all happens. We always make it."*

> *You can get a good idea of Whitney's day by taking a look at his dealings with two clients. The "Mayflower Mom" (Whitney's nickname for her) showed up first at Whitney's office. She had*

inherited $350,000 when her husband died, and Whitney was determined to get her money out of Treasury notes and into mutual funds. "I don't make my money setting up Treasurys, you know. If I had to put all her money into Treasurys, I'd be screwing myself." He presented her with an American Funds mutual fund and convinced her to invest $250,000 in it. "Did you see that? She practically sold herself on those American Funds. I didn't have to do a thing. Oh, mama. Too good to be true."

Mr. H came into Whitney's office next. "What a piece of work this guy is—91 years old, a retired union president. Carries a friggin' gun in his coat pocket. The guy's got over $5 million in securities locked away in a safety-deposit box. I've been after his money for four years now." Mr. H had come in to settle a trade with a check for $26,500, but he also wanted to know where some money from another investment was. Whitney didn't know, but he finally figured out that the investment in question accidentally had been put in the name of Mr. H's twin brother. Mr. H was none too pleased. "Whitney," he said, "I was thinking about doing business with you. And you know what kind of business I can do. Five million worth of business. But I don't think we can do business. I am very disappointed in you, Whitney." Mr. H wrote his check and left.

I've got to make one thing clear here, Whitney gave the Mayflower Mom sound investment advice. *Smart Money* had an independent expert review her portfolio and Whitney's overall advising pattern. The expert concluded that Whitney generally found good investments to suit his clients' needs. Whitney even steers his clients away from PaineWebber's proprietary funds. (Proprietary funds are covered later in this chapter.) But, would you want that kind of treatment and advice from a financial advisor? As Whitney says, "you're not hiring PaineWebber. You're hiring me." Would you take his sound advice like the Mayflower Mom, or would you get up and leave like Mr. H?

It's the Singer not the Song

Whitney's right about one thing; you would be hiring him, not PaineWebber. Clearly, you can find some wonderful advisors at PaineWebber, as well as at many major brokerage firms. There are thousands of different financial advisors out there of all flavors and sizes. And there are all kinds of titles to sort through, from financial planner and registered investment advisor to full-service broker. Also, these advisors will hold any number of licenses and degrees allowing them to sell certain kinds of investments but not others. You can see how it can become confusing.

The following are a few examples of some terms you may run across:

CFP. Certified financial planner. The Certified Financial Planner Board of Standards in Denver issues these credentials to those who have passed the 10-hour CFP exam and agreed to abide by their code of ethics. Although this certificate isn't as prestigious as others, its recipients are very serious about their profession.

CLU. Chartered life underwriter. The American College in Bryn Mawr, Pennsylvania issues this designation to applicants, mostly life insurance agents, with three years experience and ten college-level courses who sign the CLU code of ethics. Agents can also acquire a ChFC, Chartered Financial Consultant, certificate by taking three more courses.

MBA. Master of business administration. This degree normally provides a good, solid background for financial occupations.

Registered Representative. This is a stockbroker who has successfully completed the necessary exams approved by the National Association of Securities Dealers. These tests don't include a specific financial-planning component.

General Securities Representative, Series 7. This registration qualifies a candidate for the solicitation, purchase, and/or sale of corporate securities, municipal securities, options, direct participation programs, and investment company products/variable contracts.

General Securities Principal, Series 24. This examination qualifies individuals who are required to register as general securities principals in order to manage or supervise the member's investment banking or securities business (including sales supervision) for corporate securities, direct participation programs, and investment company products/variable contracts.

Direct Participation Programs Limited Principal, Series 39.
This qualifies an individual who will function as a principal for
the solicitation, purchase, and/or sale of programs which
provide for flow-through tax consequences such as oil and gas
programs, real estate programs, and S corporation offerings.

But you don't need to know what all the titles mean, and you certainly don't need to
know what all the licenses mean. You need to know what types of investments a potential advisor can sell you and, just as important, whether you feel comfortable dealing
with a particular type of advisor.

Don't feel like you have to pick the first one you go see, and don't be afraid to get up
and leave if you're uncomfortable. If you meet with an advisor and all he or she is
licensed to sell is insurance, guess what he or she is likely to tell you will meet all your
needs?

Picking an advisor is one of the few times in investing when you should listen to every
one of your instincts and feelings. You need to feel that you've made the right choice
and that your advisor is really looking out for your best interests, not his or hers. You
want someone who listens to you and offers you choices from the whole investment
spectrum, not one or two areas that he or she happens to be licensed in.

Keep in mind the following three points when you're choosing a financial advisor:

- *Don't agree to buy anything you hear about in a cold call.*
  If some of you have escaped cold-calling, unsolicited and generally unwanted
  calls by someone trying to sell you something, I want to know your secret. It's
  commonplace now for financial advisors of all sorts to call lists of people to
  ferret out potential investors. There's one question you should ask yourself
  about a cold-caller: "How could they know what's best for me?" The answer
  to that question tells you all you need to know about my view of cold-callers
  and their products.

- *If an advisor is ever condescending or patronizing to you, fire them.*
  No second chance, no apologies accepted. If an advisor can't even pretend to be
  courteous enough to take you seriously, take your money elsewhere. Hopefully you'll find this out before investing with someone, but if someone does
  sneak under your radar and take you by surprise (like the advisor who told a
  woman who's now one of my clients, "It's not important that you understand.
  It's important that I understand."), find someone new to invest with. Personally, if that ever happened to me, I'd kick the guy into next year.

- *If you don't understand something, it's shame on them, not shame on you.*

  Plain and simple, it's an advisor's job to make sure you understand all your investment options and choices. If your advisor doesn't do it, he or she isn't living up to his or her end of the bargain. Don't be afraid to ask questions, and if the planner doesn't want to take the time to explain the answers—you guessed it—fire them.

PROPRIETARY FUNDS

Many brokerage firms sell their own mutual funds in addition to selling the mutual funds run and managed by mutual fund companies. Brokerage firms sell these funds because they allow the firms to keep all the money in-house, and they get the lion's share of fees generated by the fund.

> **PROPRIETARY FUNDS** are mutual funds set up and run primarily by major brokerage firms.

Unfortunately, these proprietary funds don't always live up to the expectations you would have for other mutual funds. Even more unfortunately, many brokers push proprietary funds because a lot of brokerage firms offer extra incentives to their brokers for selling the proprietary funds. If that's not enough to make you think twice, you should also consider that proprietary funds are nontransferable. That means you can't switch them to a different company.

For example, if you moved from Denver to St. Louis and wanted to move your investment portfolio from Dean Witter to A.G. Edwards because you liked the Edwards staff better in St. Louis, you'd have to sell any Dean Witter proprietary funds that you owned. You might think that's no big deal; you sell your funds, get your money, and buy new funds through your new advisor.

What if the market's down, though, and you have to sell at a loss? For that matter, what if the market's up and you have to take a big tax hit if you sell? Add in any fees you might have to pay to sell your fund, and you begin to see the true nature of proprietary funds—great for the brokerage firm, often not so great for the investor.

Think about it. When a good financial advisor recommends mutual funds, he or she picks and chooses the best funds from all the funds out there: small cap from one company, bond funds from another, and international from yet a third. When brokers push proprietary funds, though, they're basically telling you that their company offers the best mutual fund in every category. They may indeed have some good ones, but how can they be the best in everything? You should think long and hard before buying any proprietary fund, and make your advisor explain to you why it is the best fund for you. Also, never feel uncomfortable about doing some investigating on your own.

FEE STRUCTURE

There are several ways your financial advisor can charge for services: commission on a per transaction basis, consulting fees, charges for creating a certified financial plan, or a flat percentage of your assets that he or she manages. Make sure you ask and understand how your advisor is getting paid. Reputable advisors will have no trouble telling you because they know they're providing you a valuable service for your money. If the person you're meeting with seems evasive regarding fees and doesn't disclose costs, seek help elsewhere. A simple way to deal with this issue is to ask the advisor, "How do you get paid?" Again, this is a sensible, routine question and shouldn't be offensive to any reliable and trustworthy advisor. Good advice and good service deserve payment. You shouldn't expect your investment advisor to be a volunteer.

MAKING YOUR CHOICE

When it comes down to it, it's your money. You need to find an advisor you're happy with. Some people do invest on their own without any professional advice, and you can save money on fees and commissions if you do so, but sometimes you get just what you pay for. You need to know what you are doing if you choose that route, because no one will be there to offer you advice or steer you away from bad risks. Most of you should and will end up seeking professional advice. Just remember to find someone who listens, takes your questions seriously, and looks out for what's best for you, not what's best for him or her.

CLASS NOTES

Marie knew that she wanted to reorganize her investments before she even came to class. She is a 39-year-old lawyer who just got divorced. She and her husband had no children, and Marie receives no spousal support. She makes $67,000 a year and contributes 10% of her salary to her firm's 401(k) plan. Her assets after the divorce total $45,000 cash in a money market and $150,000 in various mutual funds. Marie's husband had managed the finances during their marriage, and Marie wanted to find her own advisor to help her plot a new investment strategy.

Marie works across the street from a big brokerage firm, and one day she went over there on her lunch hour. The receptionist showed her right in, and a broker greeted her with a hearty handshake. After they introduced themselves, he got down to business, scribbling down the answers to the questions he fired at Marie.

"How much do you make?"

"$67,000."

"Marital status?"

"Divorced."

"Kids?"

"No, we. . . "

"Own or rent?"

"I own my house."

"Any other assets?"

"Yes, I have $45,000 in cash in a money market, and $150,000 in a few mutual funds." The broker stopped for a moment to think.

"OK, this is what we'll do. We'll put your cash to work and sell that mutual fund. Then we'll split the money up between a growth & income fund and an aggressive growth fund. In fact, my firm runs a couple of excellent funds that'll be perfect for you."

"What about my 401(k) at work?" Marie asked.

"Yeah, do that too," he said. "Pick the growth & income fund."

"Are you sure these are right for me?" Marie asked.

"Trust me," he said. "I've been doing this for years. I know how to make you money."

By this point Marie had had more than enough. "I'll have to think about it," she said as she got up to leave. But she already knew she wouldn't be coming back there. This guy made her sick. She spent more time filling out her daily time sheet.

That's how Marie ended up at my class. Marie didn't know where to turn next, but a friend of hers had taken the class and suggested that Marie come to see me.

"Karen told me that you really listen," Marie said when she came to my office after the class. "And I liked what you had to say at class."

"Thanks," I said, "I really believe that I can't help you invest unless I know you and know your investment goals." Then I sat back and let Marie tell me about herself and her situation. When she was finished we looked at her mutual fund and 401(k) statements together. It was clear that she understood money and had some ideas of her own, so I asked her, "What kind of financial goals do you have in mind?"

Marie stopped for a minute, then a big smile spread across her face. "I like your style," she said.

10 Getting *to Know* YOURSELF

By now, you should be familiar with the range of investments available. Still, you may not be ready to leap into the market. This chapter will help you learn more about yourself and the types of investments that you're most comfortable handling.

The first tool is a totally unscientific risk analysis questionnaire that will enable you to determine your risk tolerance. It will help you to decide what investments best fit with your investment personality.

Both the second and third tools will help you think about retirement. One assesses your knowledge about investing for retirement, and the other provides a retirement planning worksheet. The retirement worksheet will give you a realistic view of what *your* retirement picture will look like, let you know of any shortfalls, and tell you how much you may need to save each year to make sure you reach your retirement goals.

RISK QUESTIONNAIRE

1. How much short-term loss in account value can you stand?

   None   (0)
   up to 10%   (1)
   10–20%   (2)
   20–30%   (3)
   30% and above   (4)

2. Would you accept more volatility if your investments weren't going to be used for 5 or more years?

   ____ yes (2)   ____ no (1)

3. What is your investment time horizon?

   1–5 years   (1)
   5–10 years   (2)
   10 or more years   (3)

4. Do you feel that your retirement investments should be conservatively invested?

   ____ yes (1)   ____ no (2)

5. How many years are you from retirement?

   1–5   (1)
   5–10   (2)
   10 or more   (3)

6. Which do you feel is more important?

   Minimizing downside risk   (1)
   Maximizing upside return   (2)

7. Is it important to you that all of your investments are federally insured?

   ____ yes (1)   ____ no (2)

8. What percentage of your holdings do you feel you need to leave liquid (money markets, saving accounts, cash equivalents, and so on)?

0–5%	(5)
5–10%	(4)
10–15%	(3)
15–20%	(2)
20% and above	(1)

9. Which do you feel is more important when positioning your portfolio?

Safety of principal	(1)
Inflation protection	(2)

10. Which of the following investment portfolios would you feel most comfortable in?

100% stock and stock mutual funds	(5)
80% stock and stock mutual funds (20% bonds and cash)	(4)
60% stock and stock mutual funds (40% bonds and cash)	(3)
40% stock and stock mutual funds (60% bonds and cash)	(2)
20% stock and stock mutual funds (80% bonds and cash)	(1)
100% bonds and cash	(0)

11. Are you looking for:

Smaller returns and low volatility	(1)
Moderate returns and moderate volatility	(2)
Greater returns and greater volatility	(3)

12. What are your annual return expectations for your investments over a 10-year time line?

5–7%	(1)
8–10%	(2)
11–13%	(3)
14% and higher	(4)

EVALUATING YOUR SCORE

To find out your score on the Risk Questionnaire, add up your total number of points.

> *11–20 = Conservative*
>
> *21–30 = Moderate*
>
> *31–37 = Aggressive*

What this means for you is if your score falls in the conservative range, you want to avoid, for example, aggressive growth investments. The reason for this is that you'll have a lot of difficulty tolerating the volatility associated with this group of investments. After you've had some experience investing, you may want to retake this or a similar test because, with experience, you may develop a greater tolerance for risk.

What follows next is a series of 10 questions designed by Oppenheimer to help you separate fact from fiction when it comes to questions about retirement planning. Oppenheimer Management Corporation and *Money Magazine* conducted a recent study and found that a lot of us have a significant amount of misinformation about retirement investing. The following questions are similar to those asked of 1,238 pre-retired American adults aged 21–65 in that survey. Let's see how well you do.

HOW MUCH DO YOU KNOW ABOUT INVESTING FOR RETIREMENT?

©Oppenheimer Funds. Used with permission.

1. When it comes to investing for retirement, do you believe you should take more risk or less risk than you do with other investments?

    More   (a)
    Less   (b)
    The same   (c)
    Don't know   (d)

2. IRA contributions are no longer deductible from income for federal tax purposes.

    True   (a)
    False   (b)
    Don't know   (c)

3. Over long periods of time, bonds have frequently outperformed stocks.

    True   (a)
    False   (b)
    Don't know   (c)

4. All workers can start collecting full Social Security retirement benefits at age 65.

    True   (a)
    False   (b)
    Don't know   (c)

5. As far as you know, over the last 30 years, which one of the following investments has gone up the most?

    Stocks   (a)
    Corporate bonds   (b)
    Government bonds   (c)
    Treasury bills   (d)
    CDs   (e)
    Art   (f)
    Gold   (g)

6. What percentage of people turning 65 this year do you think will live to be 80 years old?

Less than 20%	(a)
20–29%	(b)
30–39%	(c)
40–49%	(d)
50–59%	(e)
60–69%	(f)

7. About what percentage of your pre-retirement income (average income during your last five years before retirement) do experts say you will need in order to live comfortably once you retire?

Less than 30%	(a)
30–39%	(b)
40–49%	(c)
50–59%	(d)
60–69%	(e)
70–79%	(f)
80–89%	(g)
90% or more	(h)

8. A 65-year-old retiring this year with an annual income of $50,000 can expect roughly what percentage of that $50,000 to be replaced by Social Security?

20%	(a)
30%	(b)
40%	(c)
50%	(d)
60%	(e)
70% or more	(f)

9. Over the past 10 years, stocks, as represented by the *S&P 500 Index*, have provided an annual return _____ that of residential real estate. (Fill in the blank.)

less than	(a)
equal to	(b)
twice as great as	(c)
over three times as great as	(d)

10. If inflation stays at 4%, how many years will it take to cut your buying power in half?

Less than 10 years	(a)
10–19 years	(b)
20–29 years	(c)
30–39 years	(d)
40–49 years	(e)
50 or more years	(f)

ANSWER KEY

The correct answers, in some cases, may depend on your overall investment strategy, goals, risk tolerance, and available resources versus current needs. This quiz, and the answers to the questions, do not constitute investment advice, but should be starting points for you to review your retirement planning approach with a financial counselor.

1. (a) More

    Generally, for most investors starting to save for retirement, the correct answer is probably "more." While it is usually best to avoid excessive risk, being too conservative can cost you over the long term in lost opportunities for investment return and the benefits of compounding.

2. (b) False (for many investors)

    Changes to the Internal Revenue Code in 1986 limited the tax-deferral advantages of original IRA contributions. For many individuals with some other types of retirement plans and/or those above certain income levels, IRA contributions cannot be deducted from current income when calculating taxes. But, most importantly, investment income and appreciation on all IRAs continue to be tax-deferred until withdrawn.

3. (b) False

    In any 30-year holding period since 1871, stocks have provided higher returns, and in every 10-year holding period, stocks have outperformed bonds 82% of the time. (Source: Jeremy J. Siegel, *Stocks For The Long Run: A Guide to Selecting Markets for Long-Term Growth, 1994*, Irwin Professional Publishing.)

4. (b) False

    The latest changes in the Social Security law moved the age of eligibility for full retirement benefits up to 66 starting in 2005; by 2022, the eligibility age will have increased to 67.

5. (a) Stocks

    According to Ibbotson Associates, as of 12/31/93, over the last 30 years, stocks (represented by the *S&P 500 Index*) outperformed corporate bonds (represented by the Salomon Brothers Long-Term High Grade Corporate Bond Index), which in turn, outperformed 5-year maturity U.S. Treasury notes, which outperformed Treasury bills and CDs. Returns on art placed seventh behind gold. CDs may offer fixed rates of return and may be insured by the F.D.I.C.; U.S. Treasury notes and bills are guaranteed as to payment of principal and interest; stocks are not guaranteed, and their prices fluctuate. The past performance of stocks and bonds is no guarantee of future results, of course, and you cannot directly invest in stock or bond indexes.

6. (e) 50–59%

Based on 1991 Life Tables produced by the National Center for Health Statistics, approximately 59% of all Americans turning 65 this year can expect to live to be 80 years old. Specifically, the percentage for females equals approximately 67% and for males approximately 51%.

7. (f) 70–80%

Government, private, and academic sector estimates of income replacement rates at retirement range from 50% to 90% of pre-retirement income, but most studies—including a 1993 study by the WEFA Group and A.D. Little for Oppenheimer Management—peg the range at 70% to 80%.

8. (b) 30%

According to the pay scale ranges and replacement figures established by the Social Security Administration, a person retiring this year who has an annual income of $50,000 can expect roughly 30%, or $15,000, to be replaced by Social Security payments.

9. (d) over three times as great as that of residential real estate

According to data from Morgan Stanley Research, as of 8/2/94, over the decade 1983–1993, stocks, represented by the *S&P 500 Index*, have provided an average annual return equal to 15%, while residential housing has provided an average annual return over the same period equal to 4.4%.

10. (b) 10–19 years

The "Rule of 72" is a convenient tool for figuring out both gain and loss over time. To find out how long it will take to double or halve your money at a certain rate, divide 72 by the rate. In this example, 72 divided by 4 equals 18; therefore, it will take approximately 18 years of 4% inflation to cut your buying power in half. Please note, however, that the "Rule of 72" assumes the compounding of an investment at a fixed rate of return over time, but the returns of most investments fluctuate so that the time it takes for investments to double in value cannot be predicted.

EVALUATING YOUR SCORE

8-10 correct:
You've really got a handle on many of the important concepts relating to investing for retirement. If you haven't done so already, you should consider updating your retirement portfolio on an annual basis, either on your own or with the help of a financial advisor.

6-7 correct:
Believe it or not, you're still doing better than most Americans. This doesn't mean you can sit back and relax. Take the time now to narrow your existing retirement and investing knowledge gaps and, with your financial advisor, adjust your retirement investments accordingly.

5 or less correct:
Well, you've got a lot to learn about retirement. If you are like most Americans, you probably haven't been saving as much as you should or investing it as well as you could. Taking the first step—talking to a professional financial advisor—can help you figure things out.

The final worksheet I'd like you to complete gives you specific information to help you know where you stand regarding your retirement assets. It's a little more work than the two you've just completed, but if that work gets you on the right track toward retirement planning, it will be well worth the effort. As I've said earlier, one of our greatest fears is outliving our retirement assets. This worksheet gives you an easy-to-use tool to take steps toward overcoming that fear.

This worksheet uses the following list of conservative presumptions to help you calculate what you'd need to do to retire at age 55 and keep your current standard of living: women will live to 94; Social Security benefits begin at age 62 (you will receive a larger check if you work until age 65); inflation is pegged at 4%, and your return at a modest 8% (about the historical average for a conservative mix of stocks and bonds). If your investments beat inflation by more than 4%, then you may be able to retire before age 55 and live more comfortably than you imagined.

RETIREMENT WORKSHEET

©Oppenheimer Funds. Used with permission.

1. **Annual retirement income desired:** _____
   (You'll need roughly 80% of your current
   income to maintain your present living
   standard.)

2. **Annual Social Security benefit:** _____
   (Benefits start at age 62. Enter $11,011
   if your income is $57,600 or more; enter
   $9,580 if you make between $30,000 and
   $57,599. For a more precise projection,
   call Social Security at 800-772-1213.)

3. **Annual pension income:** _____
   (For a rough approximation, multiply your
   salary by the number of years of service
   you expect to have at retirement. Then
   multiply that result by 0.012. For a more
   accurate guide, ask your company's benefits
   office to estimate your pension in 1996 dollars.)

4. **Retirement income needed from savings:** _____
   (Line 1 minus the total of lines 2 and 3)

5. **Future value of additional income needed:** _____
   (Line 4 times factor A below)

6. **Amount needed at retirement to generate** _____
   extra income:
   (Line 5 times factor D below)

7. **Future value of what you've already saved:** _____
   (Total of A, B, & C times factor B)

| A. IRAs, SEPs and Keoghs | B. Vested amounts in employer plans such as 401(k)s, 403(b)s, and profit-sharing accounts | C. All other investments including savings accounts, CDs, mutual funds, stocks, and bonds | Factor B |

(_____ + _____ + _____) x _____ = _____

8. **Total retirement capital you need to accumulate:**
   (Line 6 minus line 7)   _____

9. **Annual savings needed to reach your retirement goal:**
   (Line 8 times factor C)   _____

10. **What you must save each year until retirement:**
    (Line 9 minus the annual sum you expect your employer to contribute to your company plan)   _____

Years to Retirement	2	3	4	5	6	8	10	12	14	16	18	20	25	30
Factor A	1.08	1.12	1.17	1.22	1.27	1.37	1.48	1.60	1.73	1.87	2.03	2.19	2.67	3.24
Factor B	1.17	1.26	1.36	1.47	1.59	1.85	2.16	2.52	2.94	3.43	4.00	4.66	6.85	10.06
Factor C	0.481	0.308	0.222	0.170	0.136	0.094	0.069	0.053	0.041	0.033	0.027	0.022	0.014	0.009

Retirement Age	55	56	57	58	59	60	61	62	63	64	65	66	67
Factor D	20.03	19.80	19.57	19.32	19.06	18.79	18.52	18.23	17.93	17.62	17.30	16.96	16.62

Remember, these exercises are general guidelines, but you can use the information to start making your own action plan.

If you are pleased with the results, good for you, but don't get too complacent. I've never had any of my clients complain that they've had too much money in retirement. Conversely, if your numbers look bad, don't give up. Just try to do as much as you can and add more to your retirement portfolio as your financial circumstances allow. Remember, pay yourself first.

CLASS NOTES

Now that you've found out a little bit more about yourself, let's take a look at how the people you read about in preceding chapters built their financial portfolios. It's important for you to understand first that these are just examples to show you how these people organized their investments around their own goals and outlooks. The worst thing you could do would be to say, "Oh, I'm just like Carol. I'll invest just like she did." Carol's investments fit Carol. You need to make sure your investments fit you. The only way you can do that is to seriously examine your own goals and comfort levels and then work out a plan to meet them.

Eileen (Chapter 2)

Eileen wants to preserve and build her financial nest egg for her retirement. She's very concerned about losing money and doesn't think she could stand to have any volatility at all.

Portfolio:

- *CDs*
- *Treasury bills*

Cindy (Chapter 3)

Cindy's main goal is paying for her son's college education. She also wants to start building her retirement assets. She can accept some volatility but is willing to sacrifice some growth to have investments that are within her comfort zone.

Portfolio:

- *Moderate growth & income mutual fund*
- *Large capitalization global mutual fund*

Carol and Chip (Chapter 4)

Carol and Chip want to invest for their retirement. They're willing to accept some volatility, but even with their 15–20 year time line, they'd prefer to stick with large, established companies rather than highly aggressive small capitalization companies.

Diversified stock portfolio:

- *Domestic large capitalization companies*
- *Foreign large capitalization companies*

Clara (Chapter 5)

Clara is retired and wants to increase her current income. She also wants to be sure she preserves her capital.

Portfolio of short to intermediate term:

- *AAA corporate bonds*
- *Government bonds*
- *Global bonds*
- *CDs*
- *Treasury bills*

Peggy (Chapter 6)

Peggy wants to retire early. She has no problem with volatile investments and is willing to take well-informed risks.

Portfolio:

- *Aggressive growth small capitalization mutual funds*
- *Aggressive growth international mutual funds*

Donna, Dennis, and Amanda (Chapter 7)

Donna, Dennis, and Amanda all want to invest for their retirements. Donna and Dennis can stand some volatility but don't want to go overboard. Amanda is comfortable buying volatile investments for the long haul.

Donna and Dennis's portfolio:

- *Donna participates fully in her hospital's retirement plan.*
- *Dennis participates currently in his company retirement plan. He will shift his contributions into more aggressive investments.*
- *Moderate growth & income mutual fund*
- *International growth mutual fund*
- *Aggressive growth mutual fund (foreign and domestic)*

Amanda's portfolio:

- *Full participation in her company's 401(k) plan when eligible*
- *Aggressive growth mutual fund with $25 a month investment schedule*

Hopefully the above examples gave you some ideas about how certain investments may fit in designing a portfolio to reach a specific financial goal. As you've seen, "one size *doesn't* fit all" in the investment world. The single most important thing to do is to think about your financial goals. Most of us spend more time planning a vacation than planning for retirement. Once you've decided your financial goals, consider your risk tolerance and time horizon, implement a plan, and stick to it.

11 Investing Online

I have to confess that my idea of high tech is trying to learn how to work my VCR. However, my co-writer is experienced in this field, and I plan to bring myself up to speed quickly along with you.

If you're already using the Internet or an online service, you probably know how easy it is to be overwhelmed by the vast sea of information available. If you're not using the Internet, you're missing out on some great resources. The Internet's world-wide network of computers is not just for computer nerds. With a little bit of knowledge and an idea of what you want, anyone can "surf the net." If you take the plunge, you'll find everything out there from stock quotes and company profiles to market analyses and actual investment trading. Soon the Internet will be so mainstream that if you can do something in person or find it in print, you will be able to do it or read it on the Internet—all from the comfort of your home or office.

WHAT'S OUT THERE

On the Internet, you'll find information, information, and more information. If you want it, it's out there somewhere. For investors, that includes stock market data, bond and mutual fund updates, company profiles, financial news and analyses, and news groups where you can share information and ideas with other investors. You can even buy and sell investments over the Internet and through online services. The key is knowing how to find what you want.

SURFERS BEWARE

Before explaining how to navigate the online investing world, some caveats are in order. While every investor should find and digest as much information as she can, keep in mind that the Internet provides only information, and no personal touches or advice. This problem isn't really a problem if you only want to use the Internet as a reference.

If you use the Internet for all your trading, though, you might miss the interaction with a human advisor. A stock may have a bad week, and many of my clients will forget everything they've learned about long-term growth and market trends and want to sell right away. What they really need, in almost all of these cases, is reassurance that they're in a sound investment and that they won't go broke the next week. You don't get any of that with electronic trading over the Internet.

By all means, go online, see what's there, and take advantage of the tremendous resources available to you; but if you're the kind of investor who wants to sell every time your stock drops a point, think long and hard before you start trading online. You could end up seriously weakening your investments' long-term growth potential and running up huge sales commission bills before you know it.

ONLINE SERVICES

If you're new to the Internet and the online world, a major online service is a good way to get your feet wet. The major online services include America Online, CompuServe, eWorld, Genie, Prodigy, and the newly-created Microsoft Network. In general, online services offer user-friendly interfaces to help you navigate through their plentiful offerings, and most of them offer you some kind of Internet access as well. They also all have a lot of innovative features and definite benefits.

Organization

The online services make it their business to help you easily find what you need. Organization is their bread and butter. It's what separates them from the Internet. If you want to know about investing, click on their money, finance, or investing button, and you're right there. You don't have to know where you want to go, and you don't have to know some complicated computer address to get there. All the online services have plenty of information available on investing, including everything from current stock and mutual fund prices to company profiles and annual reports. Most services also allow you to conduct electronic trading and to buy and sell investments via your computer.

Extras

In addition to providing links to Internet sites, online services generally provide extras and perks not available in other places on the Internet. America Online, for example, is the only place where you can find *Morningstar Reports*. Most online services also bring in experts from time to time and make them available for online question-and-answer sessions.

Chat Rooms

Chat rooms are another useful feature of online services, where you can interact with other computer users. Your messages appear in the chat room as you type them in, and everyone who is using the chat room can read them. These rooms are grouped by topic so that users with shared interests can share experiences and ideas. You also have the option of holding private discussions with other users of your choice.

Cost

Unfortunately, as with everything else in life, these perks cost. Online services generally charge a monthly subscription fee and then add on hourly charges for the time you spend online. For many people, the convenience and perks of online services are worth the expense, but if you want to spend a lot of time on the Internet, you'd probably be better served by moving up to direct Internet access.

SERVICES EXAMPLE: AMERICA ONLINE

To better illustrate what online services typically offer, let's walk through America Online's financial resources. I'm using America Online as an example because it's the most popular online service, but please don't take this as an endorsement of one service over another.

Select Personal Finance from the America Online main menu, to open up the Personal Finance screen. The Personal Finance screen offers five main selections:

- Financial Newsstand
- Finance Forums
- Quotes & Portfolios
- What's Hot
- Research

Financial Newsstand

The Financial Newsstand offers online versions of several investment periodicals. You can read selected articles from magazines like *Inc., Investor's Business Daily,* and *BusinessWeek.* Each of these magazines have special sites on America Online that you can't access directly from the Internet. The Financial Newsstand also has direct links to investment-related Internet sites such as the *Financial Times* and the *Singapore Times.*

Finance Forums

The Finance Forums offer information and electronic discussion areas on various investment topics. Each forum generally has tips and articles from investment experts and a discussion area where you can read ideas and experiences from other America Online subscribers and post your own messages for others to read. You need to note here that tips you might read in these discussion forums are from other investors. You should never act on any information from these discussion forums—or from anywhere else for that matter—without thoroughly researching it on your own or talking to your investment advisor about it first.

Featured forums include: The Motley Fool, which, while tongue in cheek, is a site for serious information and conversation about general investment topics and strategies; Money Whiz, which focuses on real-life financial decisions such as how to budget your income; Family Finance, which covers topics such as how to plan for your kids' college education; and Decision Point, which offers information on technical stock analysis, stock reports, and market charts.

Decision Point

Decision Point offers more resources than most of the forums. The most visible attraction at this site is the Chart of the Week. The Chart of the Week tracks a selected investment's progress and gives you a brief analysis. Decision Point's Daily Market Tour has additional graphs of the day's action for the major stock indices, special stock indices such as the DOW Transportation Index, commodities, the dollar, and U.S. Government Bonds. The Daily Trader's Report gives you a brief analysis of market action for the day, and the Top Advisor's Corner has reports and forecasts from experienced financial advisors. You can also get detailed technical analysis of the market at the Daily Trader's Report site for an extra charge.

If you decide you want to pursue stock charting and technical analysis, you can learn more about it from the Technical Analysis Short Course. Then you can check out demos for commercially available charting software at the Charting Software site. This site also offers links to customer support for much of the commercial charting software available.

Quotes and Portfolios

You can obtain free stock quotes at this site. The only drawback is that they're delayed by 15 minutes. For most long-term investing, however, that shouldn't be much of a drawback. You can also build a portfolio of the stocks you own or have an interest in and check them all at the same time. If you absolutely must have real-time stock quotes, you can get them from some of the commercial sites on America Online such as the PC Financial Network.

PC Financial Network

The PC Financial Network, a discount commission investment service run by the investment banking firm of Donaldson, Lufkin & Jenrette, is an example of one of the online investment services available on America Online. If you open an account with the PC Financial Network, you can buy and sell stocks, options, and money orders online. The network also offers advice and puts out Network Alerts to notify its clients of breaking financial news. The PC Financial Network offers free real-time stock quotes to its online brokerage or IRA account holders. You can also visit sites such as Vanguard and Fidelity for similar services.

What's Hot

What's Hot doesn't really have a set content. It features links from selected sites that change on an ongoing basis. You can usually find links to several of the sites previously mentioned here, and you'll generally find links to new sites you haven't seen before. Check out What's Hot periodically to see what's new, and then check out the new links. You just might find some new information or service that fits your needs.

Research

America Online offers a number of investment resources that you can use to do your own research. Disclosure Online has balance sheets, income statements, and cash flow statements from over 22,000 companies worldwide. Vanguard Online, in addition to its investment services, has reports and advice about companies and investments. First Call Earnings has earnings estimates for stocks and a guide that explains how to use these estimates to evaluate a stock's potential.

In addition to these services, America Online also has stock reports, financial statements, and SEC filings that you can search by company name. This resource also enables you to order annual reports. You can check out Market News for the most current investment updates and information as well.

Market News

Use keyword "Market News" to jump directly to the main Market News screen. Market News offers news updates about investments. These updates are broken into specific categories:

- Markets at a Glance
- Stock Updates: Open/Midday/Close
- Stocks in the News
- International Money Markets
- Money and Currency
- Commodities
- Economic Indicators
- *S&P's, Moody's* Ratings

Each category has the latest news articles concerning that topic. Economic Indicators, for example, has articles about the unemployment rate, new housing starts, durable goods orders, and the Consumer Price Index (CPI). *Standard & Poor's* and *Moody's* don't offer their full evaluations here, but you can read their latest updates on investment ratings. The following are examples of the formats and types of articles you'll find from *Standard & Poor's* and *Moody's* at Market News.

Standard & Poor's

(Press release provided by Standard & Poor's)

NEW YORK, Oct 22 — Standard & Poor's on Tuesday said it affirmed its double-'B'-plus senior and double-'B'-minus subordinated debt ratings of Viacom, Inc. and its ratings on debt originally issued by Paramount Communications Inc. and Blockbuster Entertainment Corp. (see list below).

Viacom, Inc.'s corporate credit rating is double-'B'-plus.

The outlook remains positive despite Viacom's discussions of a settlement of litigation with Seagram Co. unit, MCA, Inc., which could lead to Viacom acquiring the 50% of USA Network that it does not now own for about $1.45 billion.

Full ownership of USA Network, one of the leading basic cable networks, would be a modest positive for Viacom's business profile. Standard & Poor's also anticipates that Viacom will consider actions to mitigate the impact of the acquisition on its key credit ratios.

While the purchase price represents a high multiple for a programming acquisition, USA Network's equity earnings had not previously been reflected in Viacom's operating cash flow.

Full ownership results in a modest increase in debt to operating cash flow to 5.1 times (x) from 4.9x, pro forma for the trailing 12 months ended June 30, 1996, which represents a seasonal borrowing peak. Pro forma debt to cash flow should be lower as of Dec. 31, 1996.

Pro forma operating cash flow to gross interest coverage for the 12 months ended June 30 would be slightly below 2.6x.

OUTLOOK: Positive.

Standard & Poor's continues to view a 3.0x ratio of operating cash flow to gross interest expense as a key yardstick for Viacom to attain an investment-grade rating.

While Standard & Poor's believes Viacom can reach a marginal investment-grade rating, the potential purchase of the USA Network stake makes this unlikely for at least 12-18 months. Improving earnings performance will be a critical ingredient in Standard & Poor's analysis. Moreover, management will be expected to demonstrate financial policies appropriate for an investment-grade rating.

RATINGS AFFIRMED

Viacom, Inc. (rated debt $2.5 billion)

Corp credit rtg	*BB+*
Senior debt	*BB+*
Subordinated debt	*BB-*

Viacom International, Inc. (rated debt $450 mil.)

Corp credit rtg	*BB+*
Subordinated debt	*BB-*

Paramount Communications Inc. (rated debt $1 bil.)

Senior debt	*BB+*
Subordinated debt	*BB–*

Blockbuster Entertainment Corp. (rated debt $150 mil.)

Senior debt	*BB+*

18:19 10-22-96

Moody's

(Press release provided by Moody's Investors Service, Inc.)

NEW YORK, Oct 22 — Effective today, Moody's Investors Service assigned an Aa2 rating to British Columbia's UKLB 200 million bonds.

The offering has an annual coupon of 7.5% with bonds maturing on December 31, 2003. This issue is part of the province's anticipated CANDLRS 3.4 billion borrowing program for this year.

As of March 31, 1996, the province had about CANDLRS 21 billion of net direct and guaranteed debt outstanding.

12:57 10-22-96

Morningstar Mutual Funds

If you're looking for a full analysis, *Morningstar* does offer the full text of its mutual fund and stock reports on America Online. You can search for the reports by fund name and see all the information that you would find in the paper version of the report. Here is an example of an online *Morningstar* mutual fund report for the Oppenheimer Mainstreet fund.

OPPENHEIMER MAIN ST INC & GR A

★ ★ ★ ★	Return Above Avg.	Risk Average	MSIGX	Ticker

Oppenheimer Main St Inc&Gr A
(Data as of 09-30-96)

Investment Objective	Rating	Load	Yield	Assets ($mil)	NAV
Growth/Income	****	5.75	1.45%	3334.9	29.21

Oppenheimer Main Street Income & Growth Fund - Class A seeks total return.

The fund invests in income-producing common stocks, preferred stocks, convertible securities, bonds, debentures, and notes. The fund may invest without limit in foreign equity and debt securities. It may invest up to 25% of assets in nonconvertible debt securities rated below investment-grade.

Class A shares have front loads; B shares have deferred loads, higher 12b-1 fees, and conversion features; C shares have level loads. Main Street Asset Allocation Fund merged into this fund on Oct. 1, 1992. Prior to Nov. 1, 1993, the fund was named Main Street Income and Growth Fund.

Performance: Annual Return %

	YTD	1995	1994	1993	1992
Oppenheimer Main St Inc&Gr A	9.77	30.77	-1.53	35.39	31.08
S&P 500 Index	13.49	37.53	1.32	10.06	7.62

Performance: Trailing Return %

	1 Mo	3 Mo	1 Yr	3 Yr Avg	5 Yr Avg
Oppenheimer Main St Inc&Gr A	4.88	1.46	14.09	14.36	23.73
S&P 500 Index	5.62	3.09	20.32	17.40	15.21

Risk Measures

Morningstar Risk:	Average	Beta (3 Yr):	0.92
Morningstar Return:	Above Avg.	Std. Deviation (3 Yr):	11.04
		R-Squared:	68

Top Ten Portfolio Holdings
(Data as of 06-30-96)

Ticker	Amount 000	Security	Value $000	% Net Assets
MTC	2133	Monsanto	69329	2.20
DIS	1038	Walt Disney	65253	2.07
MRK	969	Merck	62598	1.99
MCD	1241	McDonald's	58022	1.84
TRV	1260	Travelers Group	57507	1.83

MO	540	Philip Morris	56125	1.78
AXP	1175	American Express	52436	1.67
SGP	760	Schering-Plough	47667	1.52
WCOM	830	WorldCom	45975	1.46
	617	Nintendo	45915	1.46

Portfolio Statistics

Price/Earnings Ratio:	26.32	Income Ratio %:	1.55
Price/Book Ratio:	4.80	Turnover Ratio %:	92.60
Return on Assets %:	8.50	Expense Ratio %:	0.99
Median Market Cap ($mil):	10188.89		

Expenses and Fees

Front-End Load:	5.75	12b-1 Fee:	0.25
Deferred Sales Charge:	0.00	Management Fee:	0.65
Redemption Fee:	0.00		

Operations

Ticker Symbol:	MSIGX
Fund Family:	Oppenheimer Funds
Address:	P.O. Box 5270
	Denver, CO 80217-5270
Telephone:	800-525-7048
Fund Manager:	Milnamow, Robert J. et al.
Manager Tenure:	1 years
Min. Initial Purchase:	$1000

Morningstar's online format is slightly different from its printed reports, but the online reports have the same data you need to evaluate a mutual fund. See chapter 12 on Using Market Resources for detailed instructions on how to use *Morningstar* reports.

INTERNET ACCESS

Most online services provide at least partial access to the Internet, but this access can be expensive. It can also be limited because you generally use the online service's software to navigate through the Internet. Serious Internet users should probably consider getting an account with a direct Internet provider.

As the name suggests, these providers simply give you access to the Internet. Internet access through an Internet provider tends to be far less expensive than access through an online service. Where you go and what you do with your access, though, is entirely up to you. The interface isn't quite as simple as with an online service, but as Netscape (a brand of Internet software called a browser) continues to establish itself as the industry standard, the "Net" is becoming more graphical and intuitive to use.

Some Internet providers give you Netscape or some other browser with your account, and you should keep that in mind when making your choice. You can find Internet providers listed in your phone book, or you can usually get a list through any local computer club.

WEB SITES

The one problem you might run into on the Internet is being unable to find what you want. It's almost certainly out there, but with everything else that's out there, you need to have some sort of plan for finding the information you want. With thousands and thousands of Web sites (each location on the Internet is called a "Web site" or "Web page") to choose from, you'll never get anywhere with a random approach.

Net Directories

Net directories are basically indices to the Internet. You start with general topics and narrow your focus until you find what you're looking for. Let's take a look at the listings for Investments and Markets in the Yahoo net directory. Yahoo is the best-known and most established net directory. The McKinley Directory and Point also offer separate directory services.

YAHOO MARKETS AND INVESTMENTS (SUBHEADING UNDER BUSINESS AND ECONOMY)

Business and Economy: Markets and Investments

Indices (11)

Bonds (6)
Brokerages@
Commercial Financial Services@
Commercial Investment Services@
Corporate Reports (46)
Currency Exchange (15)
Futures and Options (39)
Magazines@
Mutual Funds (61)

Newsletters@
Organizations (3)
Personal Finance (23)
Precious Metals@
Real Estate@
Regions (10)
Stocks (94)
Usenet (3)

As you can see, there are plenty of resources available to you even within each sub-category. Having them grouped for you in a directory, though, lets you focus on any of the subcategories and link directly with any Web sites you wish to explore.

NET SEARCHING

You can also use any of the Internet search engines to navigate the Net. InfoSeek, Web Crawler, Lycos, and Excite are among the major Internet search services. When using an Internet search engine, you can simply input the name (or even just a key descriptive word) of a site you'd like to visit. The search engine will then present a list of matching sites for you to explore.

Information Sites

Most people, particularly when it comes to investing, use the Internet as an information source because it can link you to virtually unlimited data on any topic and it can do it more efficiently than you can on your own. The information is virtually limitless and growing every day, but here are a few representative information sites that should get you started. Note that some of these sites offer advanced services that you have to pay for, but you won't be charged until you accept and give them a credit card number, so don't hesitate to look around—and certainly do look around before you sign up.

The Wall Street Journal's **Money and Investing**: http://update.wsj.com

This is *The Wall Street Journal's* Internet guide to investing, and it's a great source. It offers investment analysis and reports, as well as limited price updates. It also has links to get you to other sites that offer real-time investment price updates, as well as links to other investing-related sites.

The Nando Times: http://www.nando.net/nt/nando.cgi

The Nando Times is an online newspaper with an excellent section on money and investing. It is updated frequently and often has links to other relevant sites.

CNN Financial Network: http://cnnfn.com.index.html

The CNN Financial Network is a new service from CNN that offers a wide range of stories and analysis of investments and markets. It also has links to other investment-related sites.

The Securities and Exchange Commission (SEC): http://www.sec.gov

The SEC site is one of the best government sites out there. You can find information on companies by searching their online data base, and you can also read their basic investing guide. This site also has links to other sites, including other government sites.

Magazines: gopher://gopher.enews.com:2100/11/ (Electronic Newsstand)

Many investment magazines, including *The Economist*, *Financial World*, *Worth*, and *Individual Investor*, publish online editions. You can download them at the Electronic Newsstand.

Trading Sites

Even without the personal touch of an investment advisor, some of you will want to take advantage of electronic investing on the Internet. There are many sites available that allow electronic trading. If you want to trade online, you can find links to these sites through many of the information sites listed above and also through directories and search services.

NEWS GROUPS

News groups are another Internet resource that can be useful to you in your investing. You can access news groups through your provider's news server. News groups are similar to the online services' chat rooms, but you exchange ideas, information, and opinions in news groups with e-mail messages rather than with real-time communication. One caution with news groups: They aren't regulated, and the opinions you get won't be from professionals, so take them with a grain of salt. Investing-related news groups include:

- misc.invest
- misc.invest.technical
- clari.biz.market.news

USING THE NET

The Internet and online services can be excellent tools for investors. If you have access to either, you should make the most of it. Look up company information. Check the latest analysis of the mutual fund market. Take a peek at stock prices. With the Internet, investors have ready access to more information than they ever had before. Just make sure that this glut of handy information doesn't turn you into a knee-jerk trader who uses electronic trading to buy or sell every time she checks a stock quote. Don't let the instant access of the Internet make you forget why you're investing in the first place—the long term.

12 Using *Market* RESOURCES

There are so many resources available on stocks and mutual funds that I often hear women in my classes say they just don't know where to start. By the end of this chapter, you'll have the answer to that dilemma. You'll also be able to understand what all the numbers these resources are throwing at you really say.

In this chapter, I am going to give you information about some of the major independent rating services for stocks and mutual funds. You can find these resources in most major libraries and also frequently on the Internet. While each resource's format may differ, they all cover much of the same information. They may or may not, however, agree on the outlook for a particular stock, so it is all the more important that you look at more than one analysis.

VALUE LINE

Value Line is one of the most well-known rating services out there. *Value Line* gives in-depth stock analyses and updates them regularly. Many investors use *Value Line* to help them evaluate stocks. The famous Beardstown Ladies investment group, for example, uses *Value Line* to help them make their investment decisions.

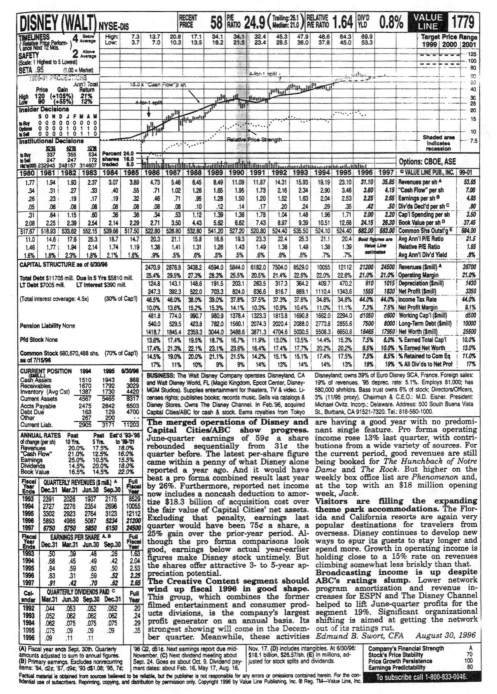

Let's look into Disney, a company that most of you know, and see what *Value Line* tells us about its stock. The *Value Line* we're using in this example is from August 30, 1996, and it's likely that the numbers will have changed since then. If you're interested in Disney, you should check out the numbers in a current report before you make any decisions.

Everybody knows Disney, and everybody is familiar with their movies and theme parks. Especially if you have kids, I'm sure you don't find it hard to believe that Disney is projected to continue doing well. Some of you probably feel like you've bought enough Disney merchandise to keep Mickey and Donald going by yourselves. Just as an aside, the pain of buying something always seems a little less to me if I own stock in the company that makes it. That way, however indirectly, I'm actually doing myself some good even if I don't really need what I'm buying. Think about that the next time you're in line for the next *Snow White* or *The Lion King*.

Value Line Reports

At first glance, I know this report looks like a bunch of gibberish, but if we learn a few basics about the *Value Line* layout, we can quickly make some sense out of it and any other listings that might interest us. Most of the information you see in this listing goes far beyond what the average investor needs or even wants to know about any company in which she's thinking about investing. Let's look closely at four sections of the *Value Line* report.

Price History

Along the top line of the page, right next to the big "Disney," you can find the most recent price of Disney stock before this issue of Value Line went to the press. In this case, that's $58 a share. One other thing to notice while we're here is the dividend yield, two blocks to the right of recent price. I know .8% isn't much, but it is in addition to the growth return which is the main focus of this investment.

In any case, the dividend classifies Disney stock as a growth & income stock and lets us know that we should expect both growth and a dividend. Right below the price listing, a graph shows us the recent price history of Disney stock to help us understand how it arrived at $58 a share and where the share price looks like it is headed.

From this graph, we can see that Disney soared from below $7.50 a share in 1984 to it's current $58 level. We can also see that although the price of Disney stock has moved steadily upward since 1984, it has experienced the peaks and valleys that we expect with most stocks. Even with the downswings, though, the growth pattern over the past ten years—from $7.50 to $58 a share—is just what we're looking for in a stock.

If we were assured that this pattern would continue, we wouldn't have to look any further, and we could call our broker with the news that we're ready to buy Disney. Disney's solid record inspires confidence, but we need to look a little further to make sure the future looks as good as the past.

Security

Obviously, when we buy stock, we don't want to buy it from a company that's likely to go under. While you need to remember that there are no sure bets, *Value Line* provides generally reliable, unbiased evaluations of the security of the companies it lists.

In a box in the top left corner of the listing, right under the big "Disney," you can find timeliness and safety ratings. Timeliness is a short-range measure of how well a stock is expected to do over the next six to twelve months. Disney's timeliness rating of 4 on a scale of 1 to 5, with 1 being the best, is below average. While a timeliness rating of 1 or 2 would be more exciting, we need to remember that our stock investment is a long-term investment. Long-term performance is much more important to us than short-term return, and timeliness is not a long-term indicator.

Disney's safety rating, found right below the timeliness rating, is an above average 2 out of the same 1 to 5 scale, 1 being the best. Looks good so far, but let's read on to be sure. If you look next at the box in the lower right-hand corner of the listing, you can find four more helpful figures. *Value Line* rates Disney's financial strength an A, its price stability a 70, its growth persistence an even 100, and its earnings predictability an 80 (these last three ratings are all out of 100). To us, this means that Disney has a strong financial base, its stock price remains steadier than many others', the price of the stock should continue growing, and the company's earnings are a good bet to follow suit. All in all, Disney looks pretty good so far.

Analysis

Next, we want to look at what *Value Line* has to say about Disney's performance and profits. In the text on the bottom half of the page, you'll find a brief synopsis of any major events or predictions that might affect Disney and its stocks. If nothing else, you'll want to take a quick scan of the bold highlights to find out what's going on in the world of Disney. The highlighted sentences give you a quick synopsis of what's happening at Disney. The rest of the text provides details about happenings in different areas of the company that we may want to track because of their potential impact on future performance. Future performance is obviously something we want to attempt to predict in making the decision to buy.

In this example you'll see that Disney's merger with Capitol Cities/ABC is showing progress, films and consumer products are generating most of Disney's income, visitors are filling the expanded theme park accommodations, and broadcasting income is up despite a slump in ABC's ratings.

Now I know we'd all like to see, "Buy this stock now! It's about to double in price and then split 4-for-1." But let's be realistic. It would be great if every stock you bought was poised to take off in the short term ("ripe to buy"), but we always need to remind ourselves that our stock investments are long-term investments. We don't want stocks that are going to take off today and then fizzle in six months. We want stocks that will increase steadily in price over the long run, and Disney seems a good candidate to do just that.

Projections

Finally, we want to see how *Value Line* expects the factors we examined above to affect the price of Disney stock. You'll find *Value Line's* projections for Disney in a box in the upper left-hand corner of the listing just under the timeliness and safety boxes. These projections are 3- to 5-year estimates of how *Value Line* expects Disney stock to perform in light of all the information they were able to gather.

Value Line expects Disney stock to end the next 3 to 5 years somewhere between $90 and $120 a share, which works out to an average annual return of from 12 to 21%. Like any prediction, this is simply *Value Line's* best guess, so don't take it as the gospel. We've looked close enough, however, at Disney's past performance and future prospects to be able to say that Disney looks good for the future, and *Value Line's* assessment doesn't seem to come at us like a bolt from the blue. Buying Disney looks like a good long-term investment.

Learning how to look further into any advice you come across is the key to getting information on stocks. You can follow the same procedure we used here with Disney to get to know more about any stock that *Value Line* lists. You can even read all the rest of the numbers in the report if you're into eye strain, but if you follow the steps we took with Disney, you'll be able to learn enough about a stock from these reports to start making informed decisions.

STANDARD & POOR'S

Standard & Poor's is another widely respected independent rating service. *Standard & Poor's* gives you much of the same information as Value Line but in a slightly different format. Again, let's use Disney as our example, and this time we'll use the report from October 19, 1996.

The highlight of a *Standard & Poor's* report is the S&P Opinion located near the top left of the first page. *S&P's* opinion on Disney is accumulate. In other words, they suggest that you should consider buying Disney stock. The four stars mean that Disney received a four star rating from *Standard & Poor's*. Five stars is their highest rating.

```
10/23/96 11:48a                  S & P Market Scope              Page 1
DSP18                           DIS - WALT DISNEY CO.
***************************** Text As Of 16-SEP-96 *****************************
OPERATES THEME PARKS, DISNEY CHANNEL,  |****OUTLOOK: FY 97 EPS ESTIMATED $2.50,
MAKES MOVIES, CONSUMER GOODS... 4/23/96|FY 96'S SEEN $1.90 (AFTER DILUTION FROM
SET UP TO 104.5M SHARE BUYBACK... 9    |CAP. CITIES ACQ.) VS. FY 95'S $2.60...
MONTHS FY 96 (SEPT.) PRO FORMA EPS DOWN|RAISED MAY '96 QUARTERLY DIVIDEND 22%
9.9% DESPITE 12% REVENUE RISE... HURT  |TO $0.11.
BY UNUSUAL CHARGES... PRO FORMA GIVES  |   FY 95 (SEP.)           REV.   PROF.
EFFECT TO CAPITAL CITIES.              |THEME PARKS, RESORTS....    33%    35%
                                       |FILMED ENTERTAINMENT....    50%    44%
                                       |CONSUMER PRODUCTS.......    18%    21%
                                       |  TEL.# 818-560-1000

***************************** Stats As Of 17-Oct-96 *****************************
 ---SHARE EARNINGS---   ----DIVIDENDS----   --MARKET ACTION--   --BAL SHEET--
9 Mo Jun    1.47/2.11|Rt&Yd    .44  0.6%|96 Rng 69.87  53.25|Cur Ratio    N/A
Last 12 Mos      1.96|Last Div Q   .110|Avg Vol   1025285|LT Dt(M)   11562
P/E             34.1|Ex-Date     10/09|Beta         1.1|Shs(M)    678.28
5-Yr Growth %    +14|PayDate  11/22/96|Inst Holdings 45%|Rpt.of 09/30/95
FV 2-  S&P Rank A   S&P 500. ASE,CBOE:Cycle 1.  4-for-1,'92.          NYSE
Yr    High    Low    P/E Range   Div  Sep   EPS    Rev(M)   Net(M)   BV/SH
95   64.25   45.00   24.7  17.3  .34  |95  2.60  12112.1  1380.1   12.68
94   48.62   37.75   23.8  18.5  .28  |94  2.04  10055.1  1110.4   10.51
93   47.87   36.00   38.9  29.3  .24  |93  1.23y  8529.2   671.2    9.39
92   45.25   28.46   29.8  18.7  .20  |92  1.52   7504.0   816.7    8.97

    Current Quarter (Q4-96)      New    Old    High    Low     Ests.
       Consensus Estimate       0.49   0.48   0.54    0.47     13

    Current Year 1996 (Sep)
       Consensus Estimate       2.21   2.20   2.38    1.90     27

    Next Year 1997 (Sep)
       Consensus Estimate       2.64   2.63   3.00    2.50     25
         Next EPS Report Date:  Late November   Est. 5-yr Ern. Growth:   17%
      Street Guidance: Buy  Buy/Hold  Hold  Hold/Sell  Sell  S&P STARS FAIR VALUE
                        9       8       8                4 (Accum.)    2-
```

Price History

Standard & Poor's price graph, located in the middle of the listing, doesn't go back as far as *Value Line's*, but if you look under the "Per Share Data" heading at the bottom of the left column, you can find the same price data we examined in *Value Line*. *S&P* also charts information about a company's earnings versus the previous year's earnings on the graph so you can see at a glance if earnings are up, down, or no change.

Analysis

Standard & Poor's analysis includes an Overview, Valuation, and Important Developments for Disney.

- Overview

  The Overview, as the name implies, gives you an overview of what's happening with Disney. Here you'll find information about Disney's merger with Capital Cities/ABC, projected earnings, and a briefing on future events that could affect the stock price.

- Valuation

  The real goal in this section is to explain how and why *S&P* rated Disney four stars and gave it an accumulate opinion. *S&P's* opinion seems quite clear as they comment: "the 1996 theatrical debut of DIS's 'The Hunchback of Notre Dame' was disappointing, but we look for the shares to outperform the overall stock market in the years ahead."

- Important Developments

  This section includes information about a $1.4 billion expansion of the Disneyland resort in California. Another item in this section that should interest you as a potential buyer of this stock is Disney's adoption of a new stock repurchase program that would allow it to buy up to over 100 million shares of its common stock. This tells you that the directors of Disney feel the stock is a good value at current prices and want to actively repurchase shares. They believe in their company.

MORNINGSTAR MUTUAL FUNDS

While there are a number of quality mutual fund rating services available, without doubt the one that I am most frequently asked about in class is *Morningstar*. *Morningstar* rates mutual funds from a low one star to a high five stars. Before we go into an analysis of a *Morningstar* rating, I want to warn you not to use only the star system rating for making a decision on whether to buy a mutual fund.

Oppenheimer Main St Income & Growth

Ticker	Load	NAV	Yield	SEC Yield	Assets	Objective
MSIGX	5.75%	$28.89	1.5%	—	$3,145.5 mil	Growth/Income

Oppenheimer Main Street Income & Growth Fund - Class A seeks total return

The fund invests in income-producing common stocks, preferred stocks, convertible securities, bonds, debentures, and notes. The fund may invest without limit in foreign equity and debt securities. It may invest up to 25% of assets in nonconvertible debt securities rated below investment-grade.

Class A shares have front loads; B shares have deferred loads, higher 12b-1 fees, and conversion features; C shares have level loads. Main Street Asset Allocation Fund merged into this fund on Oct. 1, 1992. Prior to Nov. 1, 1993, the fund was named Main Street Income and Growth Fund.

Portfolio Manager(s)

Robert Milnamow, et al Since 11-95. BA'72 Pennsylvania State U., MBA'80 New York U. Milnamow joined Oppenheimer in 1995. Previously, he was a vice president and portfolio manager with Phoenix Investment Counsel for six years, and a portfolio manager at Constitution Capital Mgmt. for 10 years. He also worked as a broker for both PaineWebber and Merrill Lynch.

Performance 06-30-96

	1st Qtr	2nd Qtr	3rd Qtr	4th Qtr	Total
1992	7.09	-6.39	2.91	27.05	31.08
1993	8.18	3.38	14.41	5.81	35.39
1994	-0.25	-5.22	5.84	-1.60	-1.53
1995	7.91	7.24	8.73	3.93	30.77
1996	5.62	2.44	—	—	—

Trailing	Total Return%	+/- S&P 500	+/- Wil 5000	%Rank All	%Rank Obj	Growth of $10,000
3 Mo	2.44	-2.04	-1.97	40	75	10,244
6 Mo	8.19	-1.90	-2.07	31	70	10,819
1 Yr	22.26	-3.72	-3.96	20	60	12,226
3 Yr Avg	19.03	1.83	2.24	6	3	16,864
5 Yr Avg	28.03	12.31	11.95	1	1	34,398
10 Yr Avg	—	—	—	—	—	—
15 Yr Avg	—	—	—	—	—	—

Most Similar Funds in MMF

Managers Capital Appreciation	Fair Fit
PIMCo Advisors Equity–Income C	Fair Fit
New Perspective	Fair Fit

Tax Analysis

	Tax-Adj Return %	% Pretax Return
3 Yr Avg	16.84	88.5
5 Yr Avg	24.35	86.9
10 Yr Avg	—	—

Potential Capital Gain Exposure: 20% of assets

Analysis by Michael Mulvihill 08-02-96

Oppenheimer Main Street Income and Growth Fund hasn't let growth stunt its spirit.

Although this fund is not the sensation it once was, it puts forth an admirable effort. The fund's small asset base between 1991 and 1993, when it was available to investors in only 12 states, allowed former manager John Wallace to move quickly among small- and mid-cap stocks with high growth rates. Wallace also weaved in and out of value-oriented sectors, such as utilities and cyclicals. Once the fund became widely available in late 1993, however, the deluge of new money quickly forced it to increase its once-small median market cap. With $3 billion in assets, it moves more slowly and responds less dramatically to its small-cap holdings.

The fund still holds to the ideal of its former more-versatile self, though. Manager Bob Milnamow, who took over in late 1995, says he treats small and large companies with equal interest. Although he says he is wary of

high valuations, he nonetheless ventures into typical growth sectors. As in the past, the fund has a far greater weighting in technology, health-care, and services stocks now than its average peer. Milnamow says he cut the fund's tech stake to just 13% recently, however, because competition in the industry has heated up while stock valuations have remained lofty. Milnamow does not allow a concern for income to impinge on his stock selections. Rather than confine the fund to dividend-paying stocks, he turns primarily to convertible bonds and preferreds to garner what little yield the fund musters. Those issues—along with a 15% cash stake—cooled the fund significantly as stocks rallied during 1995 and in early 1996.

The fund isn't likely to repeat its performance from the early 1990s, but its willingness to hold small-cap stocks and growth issues makes it a much more diverse offering than most of its peers.

Address	P.O. Box 5270 Denver, CO 80217-5270
Telephone	800-525-7048
Advisor	OppenheimerFunds
Subadvisor	None
Distributor	OppenheimerFunds Distributor
States Available	All plus PR
Report Grade	B-
Income Distrib	Quarterly

Minimum Purchase	$1000	Add: $25	IRA: $250
Min Auto Inv Plan	$25	Systematic Inv: $25	
Date of Inception	02-03-88		

Expenses & Fees

Sales Fees	5.75%L, 0.25%S
Management Fee	0.65% max./0.45% min
Actual Fees	Mgt: 0.47% Dist: 0.24%
Expense Projections	3Yr: $90 5Yr: $113 10Yr: $181
Annual Brokerage Cost	0.61%

Historical Profile

Return	High
Risk	Average
Rating	★★★★★ Highest

Investment Style History
Equity
Average Stock %
72% 54% 81% 85% 86% 73% 76% 76%

Growth of $10,000
III Investment Value $000 of Fund
— Investment Value $000 S&P 500

▼ Manager Change
▽ Partial Manager Change
► Mgr Unknown After
◄ Mgr Unknown Before

Performance Quartile (Within Objective)

	1985	1986	1987	1988	1989	1990	1991	1992	1993	1994	1995	06-96	History
	—	—	—	10.11	12.29	11.14	15.52	17.85	21.76	20.98	26.89	28.89	NAV
	—	—	—	8.04*	25.18	-6.15	66.37	31.08	35.39	-1.53	30.77	8.19	Total Return %
	—	—	—	-6.02*	-6.51	-3.03	35.89	23.46	25.33	-2.85	-6.77	-1.90	+/- S&P 500
	—	—	—	-4.00	0.03	32.17	22.11	24.10	-1.46	-5.68	-2.07	+/- Wilshire 5000
	—	—	—	1.29	1.94	3.21	1.65	1.23	1.40	2.04	2.15	0.75	Income Return %
	—	—	—	6.75	23.24	-9.36	64.72	29.85	33.99	-3.57	28.62	7.44	Capital Return %
	—	—	—	—	23	74	3	1	6	32	18	31	Total Rtn % Rank All
	—	—	—	—	46	70	1	1	1	64	65	70	Total Rtn % Rank Obj
	—	—	—	0.13	0.20	0.40	0.22	0.19	0.28	0.44	0.43	0.20	Income $
	—	—	—	0.13	0.15	0.00	2.51	2.20	1.99	0.00	0.08	0.00	Capital Gains $
	—	—	—	0.00	2.12	2.21	1.84	1.66	1.46	1.28	1.07	—	Expense Ratio %
	—	—	—	2.86	2.67	2.33	3.15	1.63	1.02	2.46	2.31	—	Income Ratio %
	—	—	—	—	137	214	209	290	283	199	101	—	Turnover Rate %
	—	—	—	0.8	7.6	13.9	23.7	38.9	164.4	1,268.8	2,465.9	3,145.5	Net Assets $mil

Risk Analysis

Time Period	Load-Adj Return %	Risk %Rank All	Risk %Rank Obj	Mstar Return	Mstar Risk	Morningstar Risk-Adj Rating
1 Yr	15.23					
3 Yr	16.70	64	70	1.34	0.70	★★★★
5 Yr	26.52	70	74	2.73	0.76	★★★★★
Incept	20.86					

Average Historical Rating (65 months): 4.8★s
†1=low, 100=high

Other Measures

		Standard Index S&P 500	Best Fit Index Wil 4500
Standard Deviation	9.77	Alpha	2.9	4.0
Mean	18.02	Beta	0.91	0.88
Sharpe Ratio	1.38	R-Squared	54	71

Portfolio Analysis 06-30-96

Share Chg (12-95)000	Amount 000	Total Stocks: 136 Total Fixed-Income: 24	Value $000	% Net Assets
2,055	2,133	Monsanto	69,329	2.20
874	1,038	Walt Disney	65,253	2.07
820	969	Merck	62,598	1.99
973	1,241	McDonald's	58,022	1.84
828	1,260	Travelers Group	57,507	1.83
197	540	Philip Morris	56,125	1.78
1,175	1,175	American Express	52,436	1.67
760	760	Schering-Plough	47,667	1.52
93	830	WorldCom	45,975	1.46
429	617	Nintendo	45,915	1.46
377	675	ITT	44,737	1.42
258	410	Hewlett-Packard	40,806	1.30
342	789	Baxter International	37,294	1.19
341	609	American Home Products	36,607	1.16
964	964	Circuit City Stores	34,832	1.11
251	430	First Data	34,236	1.09
476	476	Campbell Soup	33,559	1.07
498	736	Boston Scientific	33,128	1.05
249	443	Intel	32,518	1.03
87	415	Eastman Kodak	32,276	1.03
690	680	Omnicom Group	31,604	1.00
300	554	cisco Systems	31,342	1.00
372	789	IMC Global	29,676	0.94
497	497	Dean Witter Discover	28,459	0.90
	27,675	US Treasury Note 5.5%	27,251	0.87

Investment Style

Style Value Blnd Growth		Stock Portfolio Avg	Rel S&P 500	Rel Objective
	Price/Earnings Ratio	27.1	1.19	1.26
	Price/Book Ratio	5.1	1.09	1.25
	5 Yr Earnings Gr%	21.8	1.25	1.25
	Return on Assets%	8.6	1.05	1.17
	Debt % Total Cap	34.1	1.07	1.02
	Foreign %	7.5	—	0.94
	Med Mkt Cap $mil	10,768	0.52	0.96

Special Securities % of assets 06-30-96

● Private/Illiquid Securities	3
○ Structured Notes	0
● Emerging-Markets Secs	1
● Options/Futures/Warrants	Yes

Composition % of assets 06-30-96

Cash	13.5		
Stocks	75.8		
Bonds	1.9		
Other	8.8		

Market Cap

Giant	25.9
Large	41.7
Medium	28.5
Small	3.9
Micro	0.0

Sector Weightings

	% of Stocks	Rel S&P
Utilities	2.2	0.30
Energy	7.4	0.80
Financials	10.9	0.81
Industrial Cyclicals	14.9	0.85
Consumer Durables	3.0	0.81
Consumer Staples	6.2	0.55
Services	15.1	1.43
Retail	8.9	1.49
Health	15.7	1.50
Technology	15.8	1.46

M◯RNINGSTAR Mutual Funds

Always remember look at a fund's prospectus before you decide to invest. I know they're boring, but a prospectus is your greatest source of information for any mutual fund. You'll probably also want to look at some of the other resources I'll mention later to get a more complete description of any mutual fund you are considering. Having said that, let's take a closer look at a *Morningstar* rating from August 2, 1996.

Introduction and Historical Profile

The introduction, located right under the fund name, sets out the rules and goals of a fund. The objectives of the Oppenheimer Main Street Income & Growth fund, listed in the top right corner of the report, are growth and income. Note that the fund can hold foreign investments, and that the fund can also hold up to 25% of its assets in securities rated below investment grade.

If you were buying individual investments, that last bit about "below investment" quality would rightly set off some bells and whistles. But here's where the diversity of a mutual pays off. A fund's diversity may allow it to invest in a variety of asset classes without substantial risk. In any case, this fund is not looking to make a quick killing, so we would suspect that it doesn't take too many outlandish risks. We can confirm this suspicion by checking the historical profile.

The historical profile, located in a box next to the introduction, gives us a quick snapshot of the mutual fund. We can see that this fund has high return, average risk, and a five star rating, which is *Morningstar's* highest rating. From this glance, it looks like the folks at Oppenheimer are making good decisions. But let's look a little further.

Performance

The performance figures obviously tell us how well a mutual fund has performed. In this report, all data is through June 30, 1996. To get the best picture, remember, we want to look at the longest running average we can find. Since this fund began in 1988, the best picture we have is the five-year average. Any shorter length of time may be interesting, and you may have to rely on it for a newer fund, but the shorter the period of time you examine, the more likely you are to find an aberration rather than a true indication of performance.

This fund's five-year average is 26.52%! That looks pretty good. It looks even better if you compare it to the *S&P 500* average: 12.31% over the same five years. This kind of performance puts it in the top 1% of all mutual funds over that five-year period and would have turned a $10,000 investment into $34,396. Even a $1,000 investment would have grown to $3,439 in only five years. That's a solid return.

Risk Analysis

As we all know by now, the other side of return is risk. To get the information we want, we really only need to look at the Risk-Adjusted rating. Again, *Morningstar* gives Oppenheimer Main Street Income & Growth five stars over the last five years. This fund is looking more and more like a solid investment.

Analysis

Even though everything looks good for the fund so far, everything we've looked at has been past performance. As good as that performance was, we'd really like to know how the fund will perform in the future. While we don't have a crystal ball to rely on, we do have *Morningstar's* analyst Michael Mulvihill's analysis of future potential. *Morningstar* feels that while "the fund isn't likely to repeat its performance from the early 1990's . . . its willingness to hold small-cap stocks and growth issues makes it a much more diverse offering than most of its peers."

Expenses & Fees

Expenses & Fees are the last items we need to examine closely before we can make a decision on a mutual fund. You may notice that these figures are buried in the small print, but you don't want to forget about them. As we covered earlier, you need to take sales charges and annual expense ratios into consideration when evaluating a mutual fund. In the top part of the page, right below the fund's name, *Morningstar* lists a fund's load; and it lists a fund's expense ratio or Management Fee at the bottom of the page, fourth line up in the middle column.

Putting It All Together

Once you've read the Introduction, checked the Historical Profile, Performance, Risk Analysis, and Expenses & Fees, you're ready to decide if a mutual fund is right for you. You may want to look at the other data in the *Morningstar* report such as Portfolio Analysis, which gives you a breakdown of what actual investments a mutual fund holds and some of the other statistics derived from its return; but if you only look at the basics we covered above, you'll be able to determine whether a mutual fund's risk and potential return mesh with your own investing goals.

OTHER RESOURCES

As you start to seek information on mutual funds, you'll find a wide assortment of rating services. These include Lipper and CDA/Weisenberger. Almost every firm or mutual fund company you deal with will be able to provide you with specific information from these resources which relates to the mutual fund you are considering. Again, it is worth your time to go online or visit your local library to see which resources you find most helpful to you.

13 Putting *it all* TOGETHER

Before I send you off on your own, let's look at one more woman's experience in the world of investing. This time, though, we'll follow her from start to finish. We'll join Lynn right after her divorce when she didn't know what to do with her money, and we'll stick with her while she learns about different types of investments, finds an investment advisor that she's comfortable with, and builds a strong portfolio.

Keep in mind, though, that this isn't necessarily a checklist or a road map you should follow to successful investing. Every investor needs to find investments that meet her specific needs. Lynn's experience can, however, give you an idea of what you might expect to encounter along your own road to investment success.

LYNN ON HER OWN

When Lynn was served the divorce papers, the first thing she had to do was find a lawyer. Along with many aspects of their marriage, her husband had handled the relationship with their lawyer, too. As luck and some referrals would have it, Lynn found a good lawyer and won a fair settlement and uncontested custody of their children, Peter and Susan. She kept the house, the newer car, and most of the household possessions. She also won monthly child support which, coupled with her $40,000 a year income as a technical editor, would allow Lynn and the kids to continue living comfortably.

In addition to all that, Lynn won a cash settlement of $50,000 and a $2,000 share in a mutual fund. She didn't have a very good idea of what the mutual fund was all about, so she thought she ought to leave it alone until she found out. Lynn had an idea about what to do with the money, though, and quickly put it into two 6-month $20,000 CD's and put the remaining $10,000 in a savings account.

Lynn wanted to start saving so that Peter and Susan could go to college, but she also wanted to have some money available in case any emergencies popped up. She didn't really think her husband would try to weasel out of paying for the kids' college, but she'd heard enough horror stories from her friends not to take any chances. Lynn also really wanted to be able to afford to send at least one of the kids to Bradley University to keep up the family tradition.

All in all, for never having been involved in the financial decision-making process before, Lynn felt pretty comfortable with her choices. She hunted out the best CD rates she could find and, determined not to be a patsy for some fly-by-night savings and loan, made sure that the bank she chose was FDIC insured. A friend recommended stocks and mutual funds to her, but Lynn didn't want to take any chances losing her money. She didn't want to become one of those people she read about, usually women—especially vulnerable women who'd just gotten divorced—who took a beating in the stock market while their brokers made a tidy commission. She decided to stick with CD's and savings accounts: when the kids were ready for college, the money would be there.

Lynn at a Crossroads

Lynn was a big fan of *This Week with David Brinkley*. She liked the detailed look at current events. With all the reading she had to do in her job as an editor, Lynn found it hard to motivate herself to keep up with the newspapers.

Two weeks after she'd finished arranging the CD's, she happened to tune in to see an investment banker from a big Wall Street firm discussing the economy and the outlook for investment. Ordinarily, Lynn would have turned the channel: in the past, every time she showed interest in their finances, her husband always told her that a little knowledge is a dangerous thing, and unfortunately Lynn found it very easy to just agree and leave things to him. This time, though, she figured that since she now had some money—and it was solely her responsibility—she ought to start paying attention.

Lynn wasn't particularly impressed or surprised by anything the banker said—it's a good time to invest for this and that reason, but watch out for such and such if the government acts like so. Lynn had heard all of this before, but she couldn't figure out what this had to with her or what they were really talking about. Fortunately, someone on the panel wondered the same thing and asked what any of this meant for the average investor.

"Well, not a great deal," the banker answered. His reply left both the reporter and Lynn stunned. "Your average investor," he continued, "is investing for the long haul. Or ought to be. The periodic ups and downs of the market do not mean very much to the long-term investor. The general upturn of the economy and the stock market, and the concurrent increasing value of investments, will continue as long as the U.S. remains a strong and viable country. Despite all our troubles, I am rather convinced that this trend will continue for quite some while.

"Now is a good time to add to your portfolio, but you should not run out to your broker and do anything drastic. Wise investors should remember that their long-term return should average around ten percent, and short-term market anomalies will not greatly affect that return."

Ten percent! And Lynn was making four percent on her CD's. Something was definitely wrong. Lynn had always thought the stock market, with its wild swings and constant ticker-tape updates flashing across the screen on CNN, was dangerously out of her league. But what if she could make ten percent—and that was the average, not a "short term market anomaly?"

What the banker had said made perfect sense, too, once you got past the way he said it. The economy has always recovered from every downturn. It has to, or else the U.S. would collapse economically, and that doesn't look too likely. "In fact," he said, "stocks have averaged a 13.1% annual return since the crash of 1987." It only makes sense that a wise investment would make money over the long haul.

There was the catch, though, Lynn suddenly thought—the "wise" investment. She understood what the banker was talking about, but she didn't presume to be a wise investor by any stretch of the imagination. "It's people like me," she reminded herself, "who don't know what they're doing, that end up losing everything. And this is the kids' college money. I'd never forgive myself if I lost it while trying to show how smart I was with money." Her dependable four percent didn't look so bad again.

Lynn couldn't get the banker out of her mind, though. "Ten percent" kept echoing through her mind like a mantra for investing. "I've got to at least look into this some more," Lynn finally convinced herself. "If the kids want to go to Bradley, it would be a lot easier with ten percent than four. I should at least make an informed decision."

LYNN SEES THE LIGHT

The more Lynn looked at different investments, the more she liked what was out there, and the less she liked what she had. She bought a couple of financial magazines and found all kinds of investment opportunities that seemed to average around ten percent return or even better. The magazines called these growth investments, and the two most commonly mentioned were stocks and mutual funds. That's where Lynn focused her inquiries. She asked her friends what they did with their money and found out that some of them had stocks and mutual funds with returns of at least ten percent. Lynn wrote for the latest update on her mutual fund, and much to her surprise, she found that it returned twelve percent last year and averaged right around ten percent over the past ten years.

At this point, Lynn was just about ready to cash in her CD's and send her mutual fund company a $40,000 check, until she realized she still didn't even know what a stock mutual fund was or even what a stock was, for that matter. The returns sounded great, and it sure beat the four percent she was earning on her CD's, but she needed to do some more research.

She'd read that college costs alone were increasing more than ten percent a year, and it didn't take a rocket scientist to figure out that that was more than CD's were earning. She could practically forget about ever retiring at that rate, but putting that much money into something she knew nothing about scared Lynn. Sure she knew plenty of people who made money in mutual funds and stocks, but they all seemed so confident about what they were doing. Lynn knew that that confidence came from either knowledge and understanding or ignorance. Lynn needed that kind of confidence herself in order to take the plunge she was leaning toward, and she wanted to make sure hers came from knowing what was what.

Growth clearly seemed the way to go, but what kind and how much growth were questions Lynn still didn't really know how to ask. And she had no idea about the risks involved. She did know, however, that she wanted to find out. There was plenty of money out there to be made through growth investments, and Lynn wanted to get her share. She'd do some research, find out what was going on, and then she'd be ready to make some informed decisions.

LYNN AND STOCKS

Lynn was ready to learn. A friend had told her about an investment class for women that sounded really great, so Lynn decided to start there. She was right; the class was great. The woman who taught the class went over all the ideas and terms about long-term growth that Lynn had heard about. She made Lynn and all the other women feel comfortable with a world that most of them knew very little about. In fact, Lynn felt even more comfortable knowing that many of the other women there seemed to be in the same boat as herself—they knew they needed to start investing, but they weren't sure where to begin.

The instructor told the class all about stocks, bonds, mutual funds, and even retirement planning. She stressed the importance of long-term results and clearly illustrated the large returns generated by the stock market over time. Lynn left the class feeling that she still had a lot to learn, but she knew enough now to start asking the right questions. Growth was the key, and Lynn was more determined than ever to get in on the game. Her first step, she decided, would be a trip to the library to research some stocks.

That Saturday, after she dropped Peter and Susan off at baseball and softball practice, she went straight to the library. She asked the librarian where she could find *Value Line* and *Standard & Poor's* (the instructor had recommended them), pulled out the latest edition of *Value Line*, and sat down to read. Right away, she realized this wasn't going to be as easy as she thought it would be. She read about annual returns, dividends, P/E ratios, large stocks, small stocks, pharmaceutical stocks, entertainment stocks, stocks that had big gains since the last reporting period, stocks that had declined—hundreds and hundreds of different stocks.

She had no idea how to pick a stock from this many choices, let alone how to pick the right stock. There were just too many. And her instructor had told her she needed to buy a number of different stocks to properly diversify her investments. "How am I supposed to pick a bunch of different stocks to diversify," she wondered, "when I can't even come up with one?" The growth was there—page after page of growth charts, positive returns, and stock splits stared her in the face—but Lynn had no idea how to pick the stocks that were right for her.

Lynn thought about leaving, but she just couldn't shake the idea that people were getting great returns from stocks: there had to be a way for her to get her share. She remembered mutual funds. The instructor had said that mutual funds were a great way to break into stock investing. Lynn really wanted to take charge and start her investing off with some stocks, but maybe mutual funds were a better way to get started. She might be able to build up her portfolio that way without breaking her bank or having to sort through all of these stocks on her own, and then maybe she could add a few strategic stocks later on after she got her feet wet.

LYNN AND BONDS

When Lynn left the library to meet her mother for lunch, she started thinking about mutual funds on her way to the restaurant, but then she also remembered what her instructor had said about bonds. Zero-coupon government bonds, Lynn recalled, could lock you in a guaranteed return. They might be something to consider for the kids' college fund as well. And she wouldn't have to plow through *Value Line* or *Standard & Poor's* to decide which government bond to buy. Of course, the return would be lower than with mutual funds or stocks. Lynn decided she needed to check into mutual funds before buying any bonds.

High quality corporate bonds, on the other hand, might be perfect for her mother. The return numbers again weren't quite what Lynn was looking for, but the steady income stream could really help her mother out. Bonds would certainly be better for her than the CD's she currently had all her money in.

Lynn met her mother at the restaurant and proceeded to tell her all about corporate bonds over lunch. Her mom could buy high quality bonds that would pay her a steady income at a considerably higher rate than her CD's. Basically, she'd be loaning her money to a company, and she could pick whatever company she wanted. It was all up to her.

Lynn's mother was initially skeptical. She didn't want to take any chances with her savings, but she listened and thought about what Lynn was saying. "You know," she said after Lynn had finished, "this does sound interesting. There are some companies I'd loan money to. I think AT&T would pay me back. The phone company will always be around, and they've been pretty reliable in the past."

"In fact," her mom went on, "my friend Margaret's sister's boy is an investment broker. I think I'll give her a call and get his number. I'm going to loan some money to AT&T."

LYNN AND MUTUAL FUNDS

Lynn thought she'd take a different approach to learning about mutual funds. Rather than pick up the latest *Morningstar* and find herself in the same boat she was in with stocks, Lynn went down to the local newsstand after church on Sunday and bought herself a couple of investment magazines. She loved the idea behind a stock mutual fund (a diverse portfolio picked and managed by investment professionals), and she hoped she'd be able to get some ideas out of these magazines to help her pick the right mutual fund for her.

Unfortunately, Lynn didn't find any magic answers in these magazines either. She read all about growth, but did she want aggressive growth funds, international growth funds, growth and income funds, small cap funds, or large cap funds? And what about dollar cost averaging? She read an article about it in one of the magazines, and her instructor covered it in class, but Lynn still wasn't sure if it was right for her or not. Every article she read also said you need to make your choices based on your own investment needs and goals, and most suggested that you research further and consider seeking professional advice.

That last idea struck a chord. They are professionals, Lynn thought; they ought to be able to help me identify my needs and goals first, and then they should be able to help me narrow my choices to funds that would fit those needs. Lynn felt she'd be willing to pay for that kind of help. She decided to find an advisor and really examine her situation before making any hasty investment decisions.

LYNN AND RETIREMENT PLANNING

The next day at work, Lynn mentioned to her friend Rita that she was looking for a financial advisor to help her get her money in order. Rita said she admired Lynn's courage but worried that Lynn might be getting in over her head. "My husband takes care of all that for us," Rita said. "He invests with a friend of his from college. I don't even know what we've got, but he assures me it's good stuff. And anyway, there's always Social Security."

After everything she'd learned, Lynn felt that she had to set Rita straight. She told Rita how women lived longer than men, how many elderly women lived in poverty, and based on these facts, why women need growth investments. She'd just gotten around to retirement planning when their boss happened to walk by.

"Thinking about investing, huh?" he asked. "You ought to buy this mutual fund I've got. Up 27% last year. It's foolproof."

"What about over the last ten years?" Lynn asked.

"I don't know," he said, "but it was up 27% last year. You can't beat that."

Lynn remembered not judge any investment by a single year's return. "I was thinking more about the company's 401(k) plan," Lynn said. Her instructor had really stressed the need to take advantage of any retirement plans available at work, particularly if there are matching funds available. Her boss told her who to ask for more information, but he couldn't help plugging his mutual fund one last time before they all got back to work.

Lynn found out later from Paul in the personnel department that the company did offer matching contributions of 50%, for up to 5% of her annual salary—free money, Lynn remembered from class. She decided she needed to sign up for the 401(k) right away. Paul gave her the forms she needed to fill out and the information about the mutual funds the company participated in. "Take your time and think it over," he told her. "You can only sign up for our 401(k) at the beginning of each quarter, so you've got a few weeks to decide."

Lynn knew right away that she had to get on the ball and find an advisor. Her 401(k) only participated in six different funds, but Lynn wanted to make sure she picked the right fund for her and that her investments were properly diversified. This was her retirement money, and she sure didn't want to make any mistakes here and end up with the $7,000 or so average annual income that her instructor had reported to the class.

LYNN PICKS AN ADVISOR

In addition to recommending his mutual fund, Lynn's boss also recommended his financial advisor. Lynn was a bit hesitant, but her boss insisted his man was a great guy. Lynn finally gave in and let her boss set up an appointment for her.

When she arrived for her appointment, Carl, her boss's advisor greeted her with a warm handshake. "Come on in, dear," he said. "Have a seat." He continued after Lynn sat down, "tell me about yourself."

"Well," Lynn said, "I'm recently divorced, and I have two kids." Carl nodded sympathetically. "They're only seven and ten now, but I want to start planning for their college," Lynn added.

"Of course you do," Carl said. "What is your annual income?"

"I make $40,000 a year, and I have $40,000 in CD's, $10,000 in a savings account, and $2,000 in a mutual fund."

"Well," Carl said after a moment's reflection, "I know just how to take care of you. I've got a portfolio that most of my women clients find suits them perfectly."

"But, I've got some questions."

"That's the beauty of this portfolio, dear. Everything's taken care of. You don't have to worry about a thing."

"But how can it be so easy for you to know that it's right for me?" Lynn asked.

Carl laughed. "Lane…"

"Lynn."

"I'm sorry—Lynn. I've been doing this for twenty years. I've got the right plan for everybody. You've just got to trust me to do my job."

Lynn knew this wasn't the kind of advisor she was looking for. That's why she started learning about investing in the first place. "I'm sorry Carl," she said as she stood up, "but I just don't think this is going to work out."

Lynn didn't know who to turn to next, but then her friend, Karen, recommended that she call Cindy, an advisor she had found to be extremely helpful. When she called Cindy, Lynn found herself doing most of the talking, while Cindy listened to her whole story. She told Lynn she ought to come in so they could meet and talk more about Lynn's goals and her specific situation. She also told Lynn to bring all of her bank and mutual fund statements with her so that they could take a look at those, too.

Lynn set up an appointment and went to see Cindy that following Thursday. Karen was right. Cindy put Lynn at ease, listened to her, and asked questions to help her understand Lynn's financial situation. She asked Lynn how comfortable she was with risk, how much volatility she could stand, and what sort of return she wanted. She then proceeded to outline several possibilities, making sure Lynn understood everything she presented and taking the time to answer all of Lynn's questions. Lynn felt that Cindy worked *with* her rather than *for* her to develop a truly custom financial strategy that Lynn felt comfortable with. She'd found her advisor.

LYNN'S PLAN

After Lynn and Cindy talked about Lynn's financial goals, needs, and concerns, and thoroughly looked over Lynn's bank and mutual fund statements, Cindy made some initial recommendations. She felt that Lynn ought to keep her mutual fund. It was well-rated and a good growth & income fund. And Lynn needed to focus on growth because she had a fairly long time-horizon for her biggest investment goals: her kids' education and her retirement.

To get the rest of Lynn's money working toward those goals, Cindy recommended that she get her money out of savings and CD's (when the CD's matured), while keeping some savings as a cash reserve, and into investments with better returns. She thought Lynn should divide her money between shares in a large capitalization global mutual fund (made up of large companies from all over the world) and shares in an aggressive growth fund. If Lynn wanted to be a little more conservative, she could add a bond or balanced fund to the mix. She also thought Lynn should consider some zero-coupon government bonds to both diversify her portfolio and lock in a return for the kids' education.

Turning to Lynn's retirement plan, she recommended that Lynn contribute as much as she could afford, and at least enough to take full advantage of her company's matching contribution. Since Lynn had a long time to go until retirement, Cindy suggested that she invest as aggressively as she was comfortable with. Cindy suggested putting 60% of her 401(k) money into the aggressive growth fund and 20% into both the international and the growth & income fund to ensure proper diversification.

Lynn was ready to sign on, but Cindy told her to think about it a little bit. "These are important decisions," she said, "make sure you're comfortable with all of these options and don't have any other questions before we finalize everything." She gave Lynn information to take home and read about all the investments they discussed. She also recommended that Lynn schedule a follow-up appointment right then. That way she'd know when she was coming back and wouldn't be as likely to put it off. "I know how easy it is to get cold feet," Cindy said.

"Put me down for next Monday," Lynn said. "No more analysis paralysis for me."

14 Analysis
Paralysis

Let's think back to the Investment Pyramid from the beginning of chapter 8. The bottom section of the pyramid included things like savings accounts and money markets. These are the lowest-risk and lowest-return investments. You need to have money in these areas to make sure you can handle any emergency that might pop up. They're also a good place to save for a short-term future need. You now know these assets shouldn't make up most of your portfolio, but guess where most women tend to have the overwhelming percentage of their assets? You got it—right down on the bottom.

I think this happens for a couple of reasons. It's no secret that women generally don't like risk. The other reason is that their money is there by default. Women don't historically know much about the kinds of investments discussed in this book, and plopping their money in a bank or credit union feels safe and comfortable.

If you've paid any attention at all to what I've been saying in this book, you know you have to get away from that comfort zone. If you leave the largest percent of your money in these types of saving vehicles, over the long-term you won't achieve the kind of performance you'll need. In fact, when you factor in taxes and inflation, you may go *backward*.

Here's a real-life example of someone who needed to move past her comfort zone. The woman in this example is single, in her late 30's, and a professional. She inherited approximately $100,000 about five years prior to meeting with me. She kept every single penny of this in a money market fund. I got her to break down and invest in "wildly provocative things" like zero-coupon U.S. Treasury bonds.

She simply could not stand the idea of stock investments. When we'd invested about $60,000 (leaving $40,000 still in the account), she said she was afraid to do any more investing. When I asked why, thinking there must be some circumstances I didn't know about, she informed me that she may soon need a new washer and dryer! My initial thought at that point was, "Gee, I wish I sold Maytags if it takes that type of cash reserve to buy one." But the point is that you need to move beyond your comfort zones, especially if they lead you to be ultra conservative and miss out on even moderate investment opportunities. As an aside, while many of you may think this example is extreme, a lot of women come into my office and say, "I could have been that example you used in class."

TAKING A FINANCIAL INVENTORY

As you start to develop your action plan, one of the first things you want to do is some sort of financial inventory. Take a look at what money you have where *and* at where your money is going. As you take a look at your list, you'll start to see how hard (or how little) your money is working for you and how much of it is disappearing into thin air.

Your challenge after reading this book is to decide how many of your assets that are sitting at the lower end of the pyramid could be moved up to that middle category which covers most investments, such as high quality stocks and stock mutual funds.

Next, you should consider whether you can afford to systematically invest a certain amount of your paycheck every month in a given mutual fund or similar investment. Most firms and mutual fund companies make it easy for you to deposit anywhere from $50 on up to whatever amount you feel you can afford on a monthly basis, taking it directly from your checking account and putting it directly into the investment of your choice.

As my grandma always said, the road to hell is paved with good intentions. Most of us plan to do this kind of systematic investing, but something always comes up to absorb any cash we have on hand. By signing up for a program with automatic monthly deposits, you will be "forced" into a disciplined investment program of paying yourself first. You'll not only build a nice nest egg, but you'll also feel less guilty when you do buy that new set of golf clubs because you'll know you've already done your monthly investing.

You don't have to get involved with "Vegas Money" investments to get excellent returns. The *S&P 500* represent the backbone of corporate America. You won't find snake oil and buggy whip companies in the *S&P 500*. You can invest in moderate stocks or stock mutual funds from the *S&P* and participate in what has historically performed well—in the 14% average annual return range. And don't forget the stellar performance over 10- and 20-year periods. The same solid returns are true for many growth and income mutual funds.

Think, too, what inflation will do to your money. If you're not willing to take any action, inflation will take that action for you, robbing you of purchasing power—not exactly the action you would choose for yourself. The question isn't *if* you should look at these investment alternatives, but rather *when*. And the answer is, the sooner the better.

TAKING A PERSONAL INVENTORY

When I give presentations, I find that after covering a variety of investments, I can start to see a look of, "Ah, ha!" in people's eyes as they start mentally selecting the kind of investments that will best meet their needs. Now you need to do the same thing. That leads us to the second action step: taking a personal inventory. To take a personal inventory, think long and hard about what kind of risk taker you are and what your time horizons are. I included a questionnaire in chapter 10 that I hope will begin to give you a feel for your personal risk tolerance. I can't stress how important it is that you spend time with yourself thinking about risk, your investment objectives, and your personal time frame. Sounds simple enough doesn't it?

TAKING ACTION

Let me tell you what happens in real life, though. Most of us get what I call "Analysis Paralysis." We don't like risk, and because we feel we don't know enough, we tend to study, study, study investments yet slowly or rarely take any action. This gives us a good excuse to not move forward, stay in our comfort zone, and miss all of the performance associated with the kind of investments we are "studying." There go our good intentions again.

For instance, women don't want to buy just any mutual fund, we want to buy the world's most perfect, divinely-inspired mutual fund. We'll spend years in our quest of this magnificent investment rather than taking action and getting our investments going. I fully expect that if, in the future, I'm in line for my Social Security benefits (if there are any), I'll see lots of you in line with me studiously reading the *Morningstar* reviews, turning page after page, still searching after all these years for that flawless fund.

Whether or not you're willing to admit this, you know a heck of a lot more now than you did when you started reading this book. If you don't understand the urgency of getting some growth in your portfolio, outperforming inflation, and planning for your retirement, shame on you! And if you don't get the picture that women can no longer sit on their behinds and wait for that magic prince to come and fly them away to financial heaven, you'd better get a grip. If by now you don't know enough to take some action, it's because you don't want to.

If you've read this book, you truly do know enough to take that action and become personally responsible for your financial future. Hopefully you'll no longer be intimidated by a lot of this financial jargon, and you'll begin to see what will work for you. I would suggest to you that you put this book in the middle of your dining room table and dust around it until you've taken some action! Sure it's appropriate to get additional information, as long as you realize when the information gathering phase needs to end and the implementation stage needs to begin.

This book is not full of how to get rich quick schemes, but rather information about serious investments that, over the long haul, will provide you with the kind of returns you need to live comfortably. The next step is up to you. Think about what makes sense to you. Take some action. Get involved with your finances. You can do it—it's up to you to decide if you *will* do it.

Good luck, and remember: don't buy high and sell low!

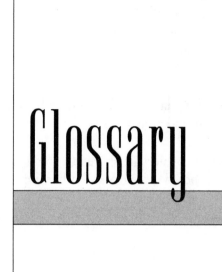

Glossary

Annual Expense Ratio is the percentage of a mutual fund's assets allocated to cover the fund's expenses.

An **Annuity** is a form of contract sold by life insurance companies that guarantees a fixed or variable payment to the annuitant after age 59 1/2. All investments that remain inside the annuity accumulate tax-deferred.

A **Bear Market** is a market where stock prices are generally going down

The **Benchmark Bond** is the 30-year Treasury bond.

Blue Chips are the common stocks of nationally known companies whose stocks have long histories of being profitable and paying dividends. Blue chip stocks are frequently high-priced and enjoy a good reputation, for example, IBM, AT&T, and General Motors.

A **Bond** is a long-term debt instrument with maturities of ten or more years, issued in denominations of $1,000 or more, which pays you interest over time and returns your principal at maturity.

A **Bull Market** is a market where stock prices are generally going up.

A **Call Provision** allows the business or government that issued a bond to pay back your principal before the bond matures.

Cash or **Cash Equivalents** are cash reserves or anything that can be easily converted into cash.

Commodities are everyday, common items which have economic value, like pork bellies, orange juice, oil, and wheat.

Common Stock is an ownership share in a company. Each share gives you one vote on the selection of the board directors and other important matters.

Corporate Bonds are bonds issued by corporations.

Coupon Bonds are bonds that pay regular interest—usually every 6 months.

Current Yield is the rate of interest divided by the market price.

Cyclical Stocks are stocks whose prices are affected by changes in the economic cycle.

Defensive Stocks are stocks that remain relatively unaffected by changes in the economy. These stocks are often described as "well-defended."

Derivatives are specifically designed investments whose performance is tied to the performance of another security or investment.

Diversifying means spreading your assets between different investments or different investment categories.

A **Dividend** is a portion of a business's profits paid to stockholders.

Dollar Cost Averaging means investing a fixed dollar amount at fixed intervals over a period of time rather than in a lump sum.

A **Double Tax-Exempt** investment is not subject to either federal or state taxes.

The ***Dow Jones Industrial Average*** is the price-weighted average of 30 actively traded blue chip stocks.

Effective Rate of Return is the value of an investment's return after subtracting taxes and inflation.

Effective Rate of Return = Rate of Return - (taxes + inflation)

Face Value is the dollar amount imprinted on the face of a bond certificate. The face value, also called **Par Value,** of one bond is usually $1,000.

A **Fixed Annuity** is an annuity that pays a guaranteed rate of return.

A **401(k)** is an employer-sponsored retirement plan which allows employees to contribute a percentage of their income to the plan, pre-tax, which then grows tax-deferred.

A **403(b)** is much the same as a 401(k), but it is for non-profit organizations, and the investments are frequently provided by an insurance company.

Fully Vested means that you've met a predetermined time period (set out in the vesting schedule) for participation in your employer-sponsored retirement plan, and all the money your employer has contributed to your plan as a match is yours.

A **Future Need** is an anticipated goal or event that will require a large sum of money.

A **Futures Contract** is an agreement to buy or sell a specific amount of a commodity or financial instrument at a particular price on a specified future date.

Government Bonds are securities issued by the Federal Government.

Investment **Growth** is an increase in the value of your investment that you do not realize until you sell.

Growth & Income Stocks are stocks with potential for both price increases and dividends.

A **Growth Investment** is an investment with the potential to increase in value over time.

Growth Stocks are riskier than average stocks, have high P/E ratios, pay little or no dividend, but have the potential for appreciation in price.

A **Holding Company** is a company that owns a number of other companies.

Income Investments are investments that generate cash flow.

Income Stocks are low volatility common stocks that are likely to pay high dividends.

Inflation is the percentage of increase in the prices of all goods and services in the economy.

Junk Bonds are bonds issued by corporations with no long-term record of sales and earnings or by corporations or municipalities with shaky credit.

A **Liquid Asset** is cash or an asset you can easily sell for cash without penalty.

A **Load** is a mutual fund sales charge.

Long-Term Investing focuses on a return 3–5 (or more) years down the line.

The **Market Price** is the current selling price of stock.

Market Value for a bond is the price, determined by supply and demand, you can get if you want to sell a bond in the marketplace before its maturity date.

A **Matching Contribution** is an employer contribution to your retirement plan which you then invest as you wish within the plan's choices.

The **Maturity Date** is a pre-determined date when the business or government who sold you a bond pays back the principal amount of your bond.

Municipal Bonds are bonds issued by states, counties, local municipalities, school districts, and other similar local authorities to fund local projects.

A **Mutual Fund** is a diversified investment portfolio that's professionally managed.

NASDAQ is the national, computer-based "over the counter" stock market.

A **Negotiable** investment is one you can easily sell or trade at any time.

Net Asset Value (NAV) is the market value of a mutual fund share.

A **Note** is a written promise to pay a specified amount on demand or at a specific date to a certain entity. Common maturities are one to ten years.

An **Odd Lot** is any number of stock shares less than 100.

P/E Ratio (Price/Earnings Ratio) is the ratio of the current market price of a stock divided by its Earnings Per Share (the amount of profit allocated to each share). Example: a stock with a market price of $70 and an earnings per share of $1 would have a P/E ratio of 70.

Penny Stocks are stocks that typically sell for less than one dollar per share.

A **Point** is a measure of a stock's value that equals $1.

Preferred Stock is an ownership share in a company generally without voting rights (see "Common Stock") but with preference over common stock dividends.

Pre-Tax Investing means that your taxable income is lowered by the amount of your investment contribution, and the amount you invest is not taxed before being invested.

The **Principal** for any investment is how much money you initially spend on that investment.

Proprietary Funds are mutual funds set up and run primarily by major brokerage firms.

Purchasing Power is the amount of goods or service that money can buy.

The **Rate of Return** on any investment is the amount of money you earn on that investment.

$$\textbf{Annual Rate of Return} = \frac{\text{(money at the end of 1 year - principal)}}{\text{principal}}$$

Real Rate of Return is the value of an investment's return after subtracting inflation.

Reinvesting means using any dividends or interest income generated by an investment to purchase more of that investment, instead of receiving cash.

A **Reverse Stock Split** occurs when a company combines a certain number of shares into one higher-priced share.

The **Risk-Return Ratio** is the relationship between an investment's safety and its potential payoff.

A **Round Lot** is 100 shares of stock or any multiple of 100 (for example: 100, 200, 300, and so on).

A **Security** is an instrument that signifies an ownership in a corporation (stock), a creditor relationship (bond), or certain rights to ownership, such as an option.

Sell Discipline is a strategy that involves setting percentage gain or loss parameters at which you decide sell your stock.

SEP-IRAs are a type of retirement plan which will allow you to put up to 15% of your total pay or $22,500 annually, whichever is less, into a self-directed retirement plan. Please note that these numbers are subject to change.

Speculative Investments offer potentially high returns but also inherently pose a higher than average risk of principal loss.

Standard & Poor's is an independent stock rating service.

The *Standard & Poor's 500 (S&P 500)* measures the aggregate value of 500 widely held common stocks. It consists of 400 industrial, 40 financial, and 60 transportation and utility stocks.

A **Stock** is an ownership share of a company.

A **Stock Split** occurs when the issuing company divides each share of stock into two or more shares.

A **Surrender Fee** is a penalty you pay for taking your money out of an annuity before a pre-determined period of time expires.

Tax-Deferred is a term describing an investment which postpones payment of taxes until you withdraw the dollars, usually after retirement.

A stock's **Total Return** is the increase in stock value (growth) plus any dividend (income) return.

An **Underwriter** is an investment banking firm that, alone or with partners, agrees to purchase and distribute new bond issues.

A **U.S. Treasury Bill** is a short-term security, sold at a discount, with maturities of one year or less, issued in denominations from $10,000 to $1 million.

Value Line is an independent stock rating service.

A **Variable Annuity** is an annuity that pays you a variable return based on the performance of your investments within the annuity.

A **Vesting Schedule** sets out how long you must participate in an employee-sponsored retirement plan before you get credit for matching contribution dollars from your employer.

Volatility measures how risky a stock is.

Who Owns Who in America lists companies that own or are owned by other companies.

Zero-Coupon Bonds are purchased at a discount and accumulate interest so that, at maturity, they will be worth the face value of the bond.

Notes

Notes

Notes

Notes

Notes

Index

Real estate, 118, 124, 135, 137. *See also* House, buying your own

information about on the Internet, 155

"Rear-load" mutual funds. *See* Back-end load mutual funds

Recessions, 52, 53

Redemption charges, 83, 154

Registered bonds. *See* Coupon bonds

Registered Representatives, 123

Relative price performance, 48

Research

bonds, 69-70

mutual funds, 90, 165-68

online, 145-58, 168

stocks, 48-52, 54, 159-65

Retirement, planning, 2, 9, 10, 17, 18, 20, 25-26, 29, 59, 68, 69, 95-96, 97-114, 129, 130, 132, 141-43, 175-76, 178, 182

company plans, 17, 25, 97, 100-5, 106, 139, 143, 175-76

401(k) retirement plans, 7, 100-1, 103, 104, 106, 109-10, 126, 127, 128, 139, 143, 175, 176, 178

403(b) retirement plans, 100-1, 139

IRAs, 7, 17, 96, 103, 105-6, 133, 136, 139, 149

IRA Rollovers, 100, 103

questionnaire about, 133-38

SEP-IRAs, 104-5, 139

tax advantages of, 98, 100, 103, 105, 106, 107, 109, 136

worksheet for, 139-41

Return

average annual, 44-45

effective rate of, 12, 15, 22, 23

rate of, 10-15

real rate of, 12, 22

total, 28, 73

Reverse stock splits, 32

Risk analysis, 168

questionnaire, 129-32

Risk and return

and bonds, 66, 74-76

and mutual funds, 90

ratio, 16

spectrum, 39-43, 85-86, 94

and stocks, 49

Risk and reward, 16-17, 40, 44, 72, 86, 89, 167

Risk tolerance, 39, 99, 129, 132. *See also* Risk analysis, questionnaire

Round lots, 34

"Rule of 72," 137

Sales pieces, 90

Sallie Mae funds, 65

Salomon Brothers Long-Term High Grade Corporate Bond Index, 136

Savings accounts, 9, 10, 11, 12, 14, 15, 16, 17, 19, 20, 21, 25, 62, 89, 111, 112, 113, 130, 138, 139, 170, 176, 178, 179

Savings bonds, 25, 65

Schering-Plough, 154

Seagram Co., 150

Sears, 55